Teacher's Guide

MEGAWORDS 3

2nd Edition

Decoding, Spelling, and Understanding Multisyllabic Words

Kristin Johnson • Polly Bayrd

3 SCHWA SOUND

School Specialty, Inc.
Cambridge and Toronto

Editorial Project Manager: Sethany Rancier Alongi
Editor: Marcy Gilbert

Printed in Mayfield, PA, in December 2009
ISBN 978-0-8388-0905-1

1 2 3 4 5 6 PAH 13 12 11 10 09

Contents

Introduction

Word Lists

Teacher Resources

Research Basis for *Megawords*

Learning to Read, Reading to Learn

Students in the primary grades spend most of their school hours learning to read. After third grade, the focus of classroom instruction shifts from learning to read to reading to learn; and from fourth grade on, students are expected to read a variety of genres and content area material filled with long words and difficult concepts. If students haven't mastered the basics of decoding by that time, comprehending the more advanced content area material—the meaning of which is largely carried by multisyllabic words—is nearly impossible. This is the reason for what is commonly referred to as the "fourth-grade slump."

Students need to have tools to help them figure out the sounds, structure, and meaning of these words. Through its structured, multisensory approach to reading and spelling, *Megawords* teaches the skills and provides the tools students need to approach multisyllabic words with confidence. Facility with these skills will ultimately increase comprehension.

Teaching Multisyllabic Words to Struggling Readers

Reading instruction for students in intermediate grades and beyond needs to be linked to the broader category of word recognition (Beers, 2003). Word recognition involves a number of skills, all of which are important in helping struggling learners read multisyllabic words.

PHONICS Some middle and high school students have "reading problems that result from not having mastered the alphabetic principle" (Kamil, 2003). A study by Catts et al. (2005) even found that decoding difficulties existed in one third of adolescent struggling readers. However, the alphabetic nature of English requires that we associate letters and letter combinations with speech sounds; when students are unable to make these associations, decoding is impossible. Knowing consonant sounds, vowel sounds, and how vowel sounds work within individual syllables can help students make the leap from familiar single-syllable words to syllables that are parts of multisyllabic words.

◀ **Instruction for each *Megawords* word list begins with reading and spelling one-syllable words and word parts with attention to appropriate vowel sounds. This helps students prepare to read and spell these syllables in longer words.**

STRUCTURAL ANALYSIS In addition to phonics, word recognition also depends on the more advanced skill of structural analysis: the breaking down of a multisyllabic word by identifying familiar parts within it. At the most basic level, these parts can be the two smaller words that make up a compound word, but they will often be syllables, prefixes, suffixes, base words, or roots.

◀ **Syllable types and syllabication rules are at the heart of the advanced decoding instruction offered in the *Megawords* program. These concepts are introduced in *Megawords 1* and provide a foundation for instruction in subsequent books.**

According to Shefelbine (1990), teaching students how to pronounce and identify the different syllable types and then showing them how those syllable types work in multisyllabic words is useful in helping intermediate students with reading difficulties. Teachers should show students how to recognize different syllable types (six distinct patterns of vowels and consonants) and identify their associated vowel sounds. Students should also be taught about the schwa sound in unaccented syllables, since the vowels in unaccented syllables do not always make their expected sounds (Beers, 2003; Knight-McKenna, 2008; Cunningham, 1998). Students can use their knowledge of syllable types as they apply syllabication rules, which describe how to "chunk" a word syllable by syllable in order to read it. In this way, students have a systematic strategy for attacking multisyllabic words.

> *"When students master quick and accurate recognition of the syllable types, they can decode words in a systematic manner.... Syllable types instruction teaches students to attend to spelling patterns in the English language.... Each syllable type gives a clue about vowel sounds, thereby aiding more accurate, independent decoding."* (Knight-McKenna, 2008, pp. 18–19)

MORPHEMIC ANALYSIS Another part of structural analysis is morphemic analysis, or the process of identifying within words meaningful word parts, such as prefixes, suffixes, base words and roots, to build word meaning. For example, knowing that the prefix *un-* can mean "not" and recognizing the base word *kind* can help a student quickly figure out the meaning of *unkind*. Knowing that the suffix *-ed* indicates the past tense or that the suffix *-ment* indicates a noun can help students understand how a word works within a sentence. Being able to identify Greek and Latin roots within a word can give clues about that word's meaning—thus boosting vocabulary—and can even assist students in spelling.

◄ ***Megawords* teaches the most useful elements of word structure by providing extensive practice with common prefixes and suffixes as well as frequently occurring Latin and Greek roots.**

VOCABULARY Using only one approach to vocabulary instruction is rarely effective. Learning takes place most successfully when both direct and indirect instruction methods are employed (National Reading Panel, 2000). Direct teaching of meaningful word parts gives students the tools to unlock the meaning of countless multisyllabic words. Teachers can also provide definitions of unfamiliar words or encourage students to use the dictionary. While providing meanings of words and word parts helps, multiple exposures to these words in different contexts helps students solidify their understanding of these definitions. According to Nagy (1988), "It is the combination of definition and context that communicates the meaning effectively" (p. 9).

◄ ***Megawords* Teacher's Guides provide sample definitions of difficult list words; teachers can use the definitions as a model for additional vocabulary instruction. Individual list words appear on multiple practice pages and provide opportunities for students to work with them in sentences and paragraphs.**

SPELLING Spelling instruction that focuses on patterns of structure, sound, and meaning facilitates efficient, fluent reading as well as writing (Templeton, 1992). After the primary grades, students have likely achieved some proficiency in one-syllable spelling patterns and can begin to examine what happens when syllables and affixes come together in multisyllabic words. They can also see how the spelling of base words, roots, and affixes influences the spelling of longer words (Bear and Templeton, 1998). Because many words are not spelled the way they sound, practicing common spelling patterns is key. Learning schwa spelling patterns is especially important because the schwa sound can be represented by any vowel.

◀ *Megawords* organizes word lists according to spelling pattern and word structure, introduces relevant spelling rules, and suggests common words for spelling practice. Common affixes and roots are highlighted, and special attention is given to schwa spelling patterns.

FLUENCY One of the characteristics distinguishing good readers from poor readers is fluency. Good readers exhibit accuracy, automaticity, and speed in their word recognition behaviors (Pressley, 2002). This fluency allows them to devote attention to the task of comprehension, the ultimate goal of reading. Likewise, students who can quickly and accurately spell words are able to devote their attention to expressing their ideas in writing.

◀ For each word list, students work toward 90% accuracy in reading and spelling. Frequent rate timings help students build their word-reading proficiency and passage-reading fluency, and students are encouraged to use list words in writing.

Conclusion

Many older students need additional, word-level reading instruction if they are to comprehend more advanced texts. *Megawords* offers an individualized program of word recognition, spelling, meaning, and fluency instruction of multisyllabic words that will provide students with tools for increased independence in reading, comprehension, and writing.

References

Bear, D. R. & Templeton, S. (1998). Explorations in developmental spelling: Foundations for learning and teaching phonics, spelling, and vocabulary. *The Reading Teacher, 52,* 222-242.

Beers, K. (2003). *When Kids Can't Read: What Teachers Can Do: A Guide for Teachers 6–12.* Portsmouth, NH: Heinemann.

Catts, H. W., Hogan, T. P., & Adolf, S. M. (2005). Developmental changes in reading and reading disabilities. In H. W. Catts & A. G. Kamhi (Eds.), *The connections between language and reading disabilities* (pp.25-40). Mahwah, NJ: Erlbaum.

Cunningham, P. C. (1998). The multisyllabic word dilemma: Helping students build meaning, spell, and read 'big' words. *Reading and Writing Quarterly: Overcoming Learning Difficulties, 14* (2), 189-210.

Curtis, M. E. & A. M. Longo. (1999). When Adolescents Can't Read: Methods and Materials That Work. *From Reading Research to Practice, Vol. 1.* Cambridge, MA: Brookline Books.

Kamil, M. (2003). *Adolescents and literacy: Reading for the 21st century.* Washington, DC: Alliance for Excellent Education.

Knight-McKenna, M. (2008). Syllable Types: A Strategy for Reading Multisyllabic Words. *Teaching Exceptional Children, 40* (3), 18-24.

Pressley, M. (2002). *Reading instruction that works: The case for balanced teaching.* New York: Guilford Press.

Nagy, W. E. (1988). *Teaching Vocabulary to Improve Reading Comprehension.* Urbana, IL: National Council of Teachers of English.

Shefelbine, J. (1990). A syllabic-unit approach to teaching decoding of polysyllabic words to fourth and sixth grade disabled readers. In J. Zutell and S. McCormick (Eds.), *Literacy Theory and Research: Analysis from multiple paradigms* (pp.223-229). Chicago: National Reading Conference Yearbook, *39.*

Templeton, S. (1992). Sound and meaning spelling. *Language Arts, 69,* 454-463.

Components

Student Books

Each *Megawords* student lesson, or "list," begins with a focused word list that is arranged according to spelling pattern or word structure. Practice pages for each list provide students with interactive instruction and practice; each page or group of pages corresponds to a specific learning step in the six-step, teacher-directed plan.

Students read the boxed instructional material on the practice pages independently or with the teacher after the direct instruction has been delivered and before completing the activities. Multisensory activities provide practice in reading and spelling at the syllable, combined syllable, and whole word levels. The activities also include matching words with definitions and working with words in a variety of contexts. Brief content-area passages conclude each list, providing students with the opportunity to read list words and review words in connected text while building comprehension and fluency.

In addition, frequent, short reviews help students remember key concepts, while Quick Checks give students informal opportunities to monitor each other's spelling progress between formal assessments. Mid-book and final review lists and activities help students retain what they have learned as they advance through each book.

In the back of the Student Book, students will find reference materials, such as lists of prefixes, roots, and their meanings; summaries of accent patterns; and charts organizing various vowel combinations. Graphs and forms are also provided to help students monitor their progress in reading and spelling accuracy, word-reading proficiency, and fluency.

Teacher's Guides

Megawords Teacher's Guides provide direct, point-of-use instruction according to the six-step instructional plan (read more about the Learning Steps on pages **ix-xii**). Clear labeling of the steps, skills and skill objectives, and page references help teachers quickly find the instructional material they need. "Soft scripting" provides teachers with language to introduce new concepts but allows for flexibility in the delivery of instructional material. Concepts and dictations are in boldface type for quick reference.

Differentiating instruction activities provide teachers with additional ideas for reinforcing or extending the concepts presented for each list. Assessments provide directions for monitoring students' progress on each word list. Other teacher resources include an answer key, reproducible assessment and recording forms, and reproducible versions of reference materials from the Student Book.

Assessment of Decoding and Encoding Skills

The *Megawords Assessment of Decoding and Encoding Skills* is a criterion-referenced test that assesses both reading and spelling skills taught in the *Megawords* scope and sequence. This tool helps teachers determine which skills students have already mastered and which skills need work. Assessment results can be used to place students into the appropriate book and word list in the *Megawords* program. Alternatively, teachers may choose to start instruction in *Megawords 1* and then select other books from the series, according to students' individual needs.

Instructional Principles

Instruction in the *Megawords* program combines several principles found to be effective in the teaching of multisyllabic words. The program:

- **TEACHES WORD STUDY THROUGH PHONIC AND STRUCTURAL REGULARITIES.** This approach stresses the teaching of rules and generalizations as a tool for sounding out and spelling unfamiliar words. The lists are organized according to spelling pattern and word structure. Words suggested for spelling practice are indicated in the Teacher's Guides, and teachers are encouraged to customize the spelling words to suit students' individual needs.

- **IS MULTISENSORY.** Specific teaching instructions are provided to ensure that students use their auditory, visual, and kinesthetic modalities while learning a skill. The process of seeing, saying, hearing, and writing reinforces relationships between reading, spelling, vocabulary, and fluency, and is a major key to success.

- **PROVIDES DIAGNOSTIC TESTING AND SYSTEMATIC PROGRESS MONITORING.** *Megawords* gives teachers the tools to determine what students need to be taught and when to advance them through the program. A Check Test assesses each student's skills by pinpointing deficits and identifying specific instructional goals. Systematic progress monitoring through use of the Accuracy Checklist, Word Proficiency Graph, and Fluency Graph is an integral part of the program.

- **IS TASK ANALYTIC.** The words on each list are presented and analyzed in six sequential learning steps. Though the final objective is for students to read and spell the words with automaticity, they often need this step-by-step instruction in order to achieve it.

- **HELPS TEACHERS DIFFERENTIATE INSTRUCTION.** The task-analytic nature of *Megawords* helps teachers adapt instruction to students' individual needs. Some students may master a word list with minimal drill on the sequential learning steps, while others will require more instructional time on each step. Goals for accuracy and proficiency are determined on an individual basis.

- **ADAPTS EASILY TO THE NEEDS OF THE RTI CLASSROOM.** Because *Megawords* is skill based and each book focuses on a certain set of phonics or word study skills, it can be used in a variety of settings and across all tiers of the Response to Intervention (RTI) instructional model, depending on student need and grade level.

- **ENCOURAGES STUDENT INVOLVEMENT.** Most students are motivated to progress when goals are identified for them. The structured format of *Megawords* specifies what is to be learned as well as the expected level of accuracy. Because students monitor their own progress toward individualized goals, they can move at their own pace rather than that of the class average.

- **MAY BE USED BY PARAPROFESSIONALS AND CONTENT-AREA TEACHERS.** Instructors do not need to be reading specialists to teach with *Megawords*. Teacher's aides, volunteers, peer tutors, and content-area teachers can easily follow the instruction in the Teacher's Guide. Instructions for how to guide students through each of the six learning steps are written in clear and simple language.

Overview of Teaching Strategies

Megawords teaches the reading, spelling, and contextual use of multisyllabic words through a systematic progression of skills. The multisensory teaching strategies for reading and spelling are uniform throughout the *Megawords* series, though each book focuses on a distinct group of word study skills. Lists within each book emphasize a common phonic or structural element of the English language. Some words are placed on more than one list, and some lists include words with phonic elements that are not focused on until later in the sequence.

Reading and Spelling Strategies

For reading, the goal is to teach students word attack skills that they can apply to sounding out unfamiliar words. Thus, students are presented with a large number of words that they may never have seen before in order to challenge their understanding of the concepts taught.

In contrast, fewer words are required for spelling mastery because spelling is a much more complex skill. Multisyllabic words frequently contain the schwa sound, which can be spelled with any of the five vowels. While this may or may not present a reading problem for students, it is almost always a major barrier for those students who must learn to spell phonetically. This difficulty also applies to other vowel and consonant sounds that can be spelled in more than one way. The spelling task is usually further complicated by students not receiving immediate feedback on their performance. For these reasons, students are not expected to learn the correct spellings of all the words on the lists. Rather, students should learn how to spell a limited number of useful words well. Common words that students are likely to use in their writing are identified with an asterisk in the Teacher's Guides. Teachers and students are encouraged to modify the number of required spelling words to suit individual needs.

Learning Steps

Instruction for each word list is divided into six sequential learning steps to help students reach the goal of reading and spelling with automaticity. Each step includes a decoding (reading) task and an encoding (spelling) task. The chart on page **x** provides a quick summary of the learning steps and associated tasks. Activities corresponding to each step are described in detail on pages **xi–xii**.

Reading and Spelling Tasks for the *Megawords* Learning Steps

	Reading	Spelling
STEP 1 **Work with One-Syllable Words and Word Parts**	See–Say	Hear–Write
STEP 2 **Work with the Combined Word Parts**	Identify and combine parts	Isolate and spell parts
STEP 3 **Work with the Whole Word**	Divide into syllables	Spell parts in sequence
STEP 4 **Work with the Words in Context**	Complete sentences and read them for meaning	Spell words in sentences
STEP 5 **Monitor Progress to Increase Reading and Spelling Accuracy**	Read selected words with 90% accuracy	Spell selected words with 90% accuracy
STEP 6 **Monitor Progress to Build Reading Proficiency**	Read list words with speed and accuracy Read list words in connected text to build comprehension and fluency	Use correctly-spelled list words in writing

STEP 1

Work with One-Syllable Words and Word Parts

Students start each lesson with syllable-level practice. They may identify types of syllables or work on prefixes, suffixes, or special vowel and consonant combinations. Practice pages require students both to read and to spell the one-syllable words or word parts. Students can get additional practice by using drill cards; ideas for differentiating instruction with these cards are provided.

Activities include:

- Reading and spelling syllables or one-syllable words (see Student Book page 40)

STEP 2

Work with Combined Word Parts

Students recognize word parts within multisyllabic words, combine them, and read the whole word. For spelling, the teacher dictates a whole word, and students isolate and spell the word parts. At first, students say the individual word parts aloud before spelling them; eventually, they can say them to themselves. Practice with common spelling patterns for the schwa sound is included when relevant. As students combine word parts to read whole words, teachers are encouraged to discuss word meaning.

SYLLABLES AND SYLLABICATION For Reading, words are presented as detached syllables as an intermediate step to help students identify the correct vowel sound before tackling whole words. Syllabication in *Megawords* is closer to that used for hyphenation than that found in pronunciation guides in a dictionary. Syllabication is presented as simply as possible to avoid confusing the student with technical syllabication rules.

VOWEL SOUNDS IN UNACCENTED SYLLABLES Students are sometimes asked to mark vowels in words with an unaccented syllable. For these syllables, some dictionaries list both the schwa and the short-*i* sounds as acceptable, and some vary on the preferred pronunciation. Regional accents also affect pronunciation. Do not insist that students know the technically correct vowel sound as long as they can decode the word.

Activities include:

- Identifying accented syllables (see Student Book page 21)
- Completing words with common spelling patterns (see Student Book page 24)

STEP 3

Work with the Whole Word

For Reading, students practice applying relevant word attack skills. Practice pages require them to divide whole words into syllables and pronounce them. The Spelling practice pages focus on words frequently used in writing. Students practice spelling the recurring phonic elements in common words. They learn spelling rules and generalizations and practice proofreading skills.

Activities include:

- Dividing words into syllables (see Student Book page 44)
- Sorting words by spelling pattern or pronunciation (see Student Book page 68)

STEP 4 Work with Words in Context

Students apply their reading and spelling skills to working with words in context. Vocabulary activities encourage students to learn word meanings from context as well as to develop dictionary skills. Reading and writing sentences that emphasize the specific phonic element in each list are also included.

Activities include:

- Recognizing and understanding parts of speech (see Student Book page 34)
- Completing cloze sentences (see Student Book page 48)

STEP 5 Monitor Progress to Increase Reading and Spelling Accuracy

When students have successfully completed Steps 1 through 4, teachers administer Reading and Spelling Skill Checks. These assessments should be repeated until students have achieved 90% accuracy or better.

Students can record their Reading and Spelling Skill Check scores in the appropriate columns of the Accuracy Checklist (page 116; Student Book page 103). These scores can be written as fractions: the number correct over the number attempted. The date for each score should be noted as well. When students have achieved 90% accuracy, they can shade in the box to indicate mastery. A sample of a completed Accuracy Checklist can be found at intervention.schoolspecialty.com.

STEP 6 Monitor Progress to Build Reading Proficiency

WORD PROFICIENCY Students' skills must be automatic and proficient before they can comprehend a passage or progress to more difficult skills. Thus, once students have read a selection of list words untimed with 90% accuracy, they set an individual goal for word proficiency and work on increasing their reading speed by doing frequent rate timings. Students can record their performance on the Word Proficiency Graph, indicating number of words read correctly in a minute as well as the number of errors.
A reproducible Word Proficiency Graph is on page 117 (Student Book page 104).
A completed Word Proficiency Graph can be found at intervention.schoolspecialty.com.

FLUENCY The last page of each Student Book lesson gives students an opportunity to read list words in connected text. The approximately 150-word passage incorporates words from the current list as well as review words covered in earlier lists in the *Megawords* scope and sequence. Students practice short word lists, read the passage, and answer vocabulary and comprehension questions about the passage. Then students have the opportunity to build their fluency by doing repeated readings of the passage until they reach their individual fluency goals. Students record performance on the Fluency Graph, indicating the number of words read correctly in a minute as well as the number of errors. A reproducible Fluency Graph is on page 118 (Student Book page 105). A sample of a completed Fluency Graph can be found at intervention.schoolspecialty.com.

USING LIST WORDS IN WRITING Giving students sufficient practice in spelling words helps the spelling process become automatic. They are then able to concentrate on the content of their writing, using correctly spelled words to convey their ideas. Students should be encouraged to use their newly learned list words in their writing.

Administering the Check Test

The first step in using *Megawords 3* is to administer the Check Test, which should be used as both a pretest and a posttest.

The Check Test informally assesses a student's ability to read and spell words that follow the patterns presented in *Megawords 3*. Although the reading section of the Check Test must be administered individually, the items for the spelling section (listed below) can be administered to a group.

To test reading, give the student the Student's Reading Copy (page 120) and instruct him or her to read down the columns. Use the Examiner's Recording Form (page 119; Student Book page 107) to note errors and mark the number correct. Keep a record of student responses so that errors can be analyzed later. Note that the Examiner's Recording Form in the Student Book is double-sided; one side can be used for a pretest and the other for a posttest.

To test spelling, give students blank paper and tell them to number from one to five, eight times. Dictate the following words to assess their ability to spell frequently used words that follow the patterns presented in *Megawords 3*.

15. *-al* and *-ic* Endings
1. normal; 2. capital; 3. music; 4. elastic; 5. central

16. *-it, -ite, -et,* and *-ate* Endings
1. limit; 2. definite; 3. target; 4. private; 5. credit

17. Middle-Syllable Schwa
1. benefit; 2. separate; 3. alcohol; 4. argument; 5. regular

18. *-ant, -ance, -ent,* and *-ence* Endings
1. silent; 2. distant; 3. important; 4. agent; 5. difference

19. *-ive, -ice, -ace, -ine,* and *-ain* Endings
1. relative; 2. notice; 3. examine; 4. bargain; 5. furnace

If a student misses the first two words of a group and it is apparent that the words are too difficult, discontinue testing in that group; the purpose of the Check Test is simply to identify specific skill deficits and to determine a starting point for instruction. In some cases, you may wish to administer the Check Test in sections as students progress through the book rather than in one sitting.

Sharing and Recording Check Test Results

Share the Check Test results with your students so that they are aware of what they know and what they need to learn.

Record students' Check Test results on the Accuracy Checklists (page 116; Student Book page 103). Record section scores in reading and spelling as a fraction, writing the number correct over the number 5. A sample of a completed Accuracy Checklist can be found at intervention.schoolspecialty.com.

Interpreting Check Test Results and Planning Instruction

By examining the Check Test Scores column, it should be clear which list a student should begin work on. If a student reads and spells all the words from a particular section correctly, instruction on the corresponding list is not necessary and can be marked "mastered." In this case, the student can immediately begin to build word-reading proficiency on that list (Step 6). If a student scores 4/5 for a given list, begin instruction at Step 5, working to increase accuracy; the Reading and Spelling Skill Checks will reveal whether additional instruction on Steps 1 through 4 will be necessary.

Be sure to continue to reassess students' skills as you work with them. Often you will discover strengths or weaknesses that were not revealed in the Check Test results.

Special Considerations for *Megawords 3*

Before beginning *Megawords 3*, students should be able to:

- read and spell the six types of syllables taught in *Megawords 1*;
- syllabicate words according to the rules taught in *Megawords 1*;
- read and spell words with the prefixes, suffixes, and accent patterns taught in *Megawords 2*.

If these skills are automatic, students can concentrate on correctly spelling and reading the unaccented ending patterns in *Megawords 3*.

Teaching the Schwa Sound

Megawords 3 focuses on multisyllabic words that have unaccented syllables, either at the end or in the middle of words. The unaccented vowel has either a schwa sound *(national, resident, enemy)* or a short-*i* sound *(expensive, chocolate)*. Some dictionaries list both the schwa and the short-*i* sounds as acceptable, and regional accents can also affect pronunciation. For these reasons, teachers need not insist that students know the exact vowel sounds as long as they can decode the word.

Because any vowel can have the schwa or short-*i* sound in the words in *Megawords 3*, students usually have more difficulty spelling these words than reading them. Consequently, the instruction groups common spelling patterns so that students will more easily read and spell the words. It is essential that students develop a sense of what "looks right."

1. When dictating words, pronounce the unaccented syllable with a short or long sound rather than the schwa sound. This technique may be helpful initially, but it should eventually be discontinued.
2. Encourage students to try alternative spellings. For example, they might write *granit*, *granet*, and *granite* and then choose the spelling that "looks right." This technique works well with students who have good visual memory skills.
3. Students should refer to a dictionary.
4. Where appropriate, use mnemonic devices to help students remember schwa spellings. For example, "An *important ant* pays a *different rent*."

Using the drill cards described in Step 1 of each list can be helpful in presenting some of the endings in *Megawords 3*. Games can provide excellent reinforcement activities. Adaptations of Crazy Eights, Go Fish, or Old Maid work well; cards with the same ending or unaccented vowel can be considered the same suit. Trivia games can be adapted so that students can choose to read a 50-point word such as *mezzanine* or a 5-point word such as *picnic*. Students can also make wall charts with a large number of words with a specific ending.

Accent Patterns

Understanding accent patterns should not be an end in itself, but rather, a means for decoding unfamiliar words. *Megawords 3* reviews accent patterns in two-syllable words and introduces accent patterns in three- and four-syllable words. Pronouncing words slowly, tapping out words by syllable, and emphasizing the accented syllable can help students master difficult accent patterns. Both the Teacher's Guide (pages 114–115) and the Student Book (pages 101–102) include a complete explanation of these accent patterns.

WORD LIST 15 *-al* and *-ic* Endings

-al = /əl/

accidental
actual*
admiral
animal*
arrival*
capital*
cardinal
central*
coastal
coral
criminal
decimal
dental*
dismal
eternal
external
fatal
federal*
final*
fiscal
formal*
funeral*
general*
global
hospital*
immortal
internal
interval
legal*
liberal
local*
loyal*
mental
metal*
mineral*
moral
mortal
national*
natural*
naval
normal*
optional*
oral
original*
pedal
personal*
petal
plural
real
removal
reversal
royal
several*
signal*
skeptical
spinal
structural
terminal
tidal
trial*
universal
vital
vocal

-ic = /ĭk/

academic
acrobatic
allergic
anemic
angelic
antic
apathetic
arctic
artistic
athletic*
Atlantic*
atomic
automatic*
basic*
catastrophic
Cedric
ceramic
characteristic
clinic*
comic*
critic
democratic*
ecstatic
elastic
electric*
energetic
Eric
fantastic*
frantic
garlic
geographic*
gigantic*
heroic
ironic
logic*
music*
mystic
Pacific*
panic
pathetic
patriotic
phonetic
picnic*
plastic*
prolific
public*
sarcastic
skeptic
spastic
static
statistic
systematic
tactic
terrific*
traffic*

Note:

Suggestions for practical spelling words are indicated with an asterisk (*). Or you may want to decide with students which words they will be responsible for spelling, and have them place an asterisk next to each of those words.

WORD LIST 15 -*al* and -*ic* Endings

CONCEPTS COVERED

- Accented Syllables
- Unaccented Syllables
- -*al* Ending
- -*ic* Ending
- Accent Patterns

Review with students the definitions of **Accented Syllables** and **Unaccented Syllables** (page 114; Student Book page 101). As needed, remind students that the schwa is a vowel sound similar to the short-*u* sound in *up*. The schwa sound (/ə/) is found only in unaccented syllables of multisyllabic words.

STEP 1 Work with One-Syllable Words and Word Parts

Reading and Spelling

OBJECTIVE *Students will correctly pronounce and spell the* -al *and* -ic *endings.*

Practice Page 15A

- Display the -*al* and -*ic* endings.
- Remind students that in single-syllable words, the -*al* ending has a short-*a* sound and says /ăl/.
- **SAY:** In multisyllabic words, the **-*al* Ending** is unaccented and says /əl/, as in *fin<u>al</u>*.
- Display the final syllables *nal, tal,* and *cal,* and read them aloud with students to practice the /əl/ pronunciation.
- Then point out that in single-syllable words, the -*ic* ending has a short-*i* sound and says /ĭk/.
  SAY: In multisyllabic words, the unaccented **-*ic* Ending** also has a short-*i* sound and says /ĭk/, as in *picn<u>ic</u>*.
- Display the final syllables *tic, pic,* and *sic,* and read them aloud with students to practice the /ĭk/ pronunciation.
- Have students read independently or with you the boxed text on 15A. Then have them complete the page, making sure they understand the directions for each activity.

DIFFERENTIATING INSTRUCTION For students who need further practice with the -*al* and -*ic* endings, have them make drill cards. Tell students to write each List 15 ending on an index card. They can then test one another on pronunciation and spelling of the endings.

STEP

2 Work with Combined Word Parts

Reading

OBJECTIVE *Students will pronounce individual syllables and combine them to read a whole word. They will match syllables to build whole words.*

Practice Page 15B

- Display the word *final.* Underline the *-al* ending as you remind students that the unaccented ending *-al* has the schwa sound and says /əl/.
- Display the word *oral* syllable by syllable. Ask a volunteer to say the syllables to read the whole word. Have the volunteer write the word. Repeat this procedure with the words *tidal* and *eternal.*
- Then display the syllables *lo, mor,* and *vi* in a column. In a second column, write the syllable *tal.* Ask two volunteers to pair a syllable from the first column with the syllable *tal* to make a real word. *(mortal, vital)* Have students say each word.
- Have students read independently or with you the boxed text on 15B. Then have them complete the page, making sure they understand the directions for each activity.
- **VOCABULARY** As students make and write whole words on 15B, review selected word meanings that they may find difficult. Use the following as models.
  - — When something is depressing and gloomy, it is described as *dismal.*
  - — A *moral* person is honorable and follows standards of good behavior. *Morals* are a person's standards of good behavior. The lesson in a story is also called a *moral.*

Practice Page 15C

- Review the following points about accented syllables as necessary:
  1. An accented syllable has more emphasis than the other syllables in a word.
  2. An accented syllable is pronounced with a clear vowel sound according to its syllable type. For example, an accented closed syllable has a short-vowel sound.
- Remind students that the *-ic* ending is unaccented and says /ĭk/.
  SAY: In words with the *-ic* ending, the accent is on the syllable just before the ending, as in the word *picnic.*
- Display the word *arctic* syllable by syllable. Point out the *-ic* ending, and explain that the syllable just before it will be accented. Have a volunteer identify the accented syllable *(arc)* and draw a box around it. Have students read the word aloud with you. Follow the same procedure with *terrific.*
- Have students read independently or with you the boxed text on 15C. Then have them complete the page, making sure they understand the directions for each activity.
- **VOCABULARY** As students read and write whole words on 15C, review selected word meanings that they may find difficult. Use the following as models.
  - — *Prolific* is used to describe someone who produces a large amount of something. A writer who has written a large number of books could be described as *prolific.*
  - — *Anemic* can describe someone with anemia, a medical condition of having a low number of red blood cells; *anemic* can also mean "pale" or "listless and weak."
  - — *Apathetic* means "indifferent" or "not interested."

Spelling

OBJECTIVE *Students will isolate, pronounce, and spell syllables that are parts of list words.*

Practice Page 15D

- Have students complete 15D, making sure they understand the directions for each activity.
- For Activity 1, dictate the following words. Make sure students say each word, isolate the missing syllable(s), and say the whole word as they write it.
  DICTATION: 1. oral; 2. traffic; 3. moral; 4. trial; 5. funeral; 6. electric; 7. personal; 8. terrific; 9. hospital; 10. geographic; 11. systematic; 12. catastrophic
- **VOCABULARY** As students work with the words in Activity 2, review selected word meanings that they may find difficult. Use the following as models.
  — When people are *ecstatic,* they are extremely happy and excited.
  — *Cardinal* can refer to a religious leader or to something of great importance. The word *cardinal* can also describe something that is a deep or bright red, like the color of the bird of the same name, a *cardinal.*

STEP 3 Work with the Whole Word

Reading

OBJECTIVE *Students will apply accent patterns to read list words correctly, with special attention to parts of speech.*

Practice Page 15E

- Discuss the following points with students:
  1. Words that end in *-ic* or *-al* can be nouns or adjectives.
  2. Nouns refer to people, places, things, or ideas *(child, bedroom, car, perfection).*
  3. Adjectives are words that describe nouns *(lively, pretty, large, swift).*
- Provide or have students suggest examples of List 15 words that are nouns *(animal, garlic)* and adjectives *(loyal, allergic).*
- Have students complete 15E, making sure they understand the directions. Have them use a dictionary or work with a partner as necessary.
- After students complete Activity 1, you may wish to work with them to identify which words in that activity are nouns and which words are adjectives. *(nouns: pedal, signal, critic, antic, panic, tactic, and petal; adjectives: spastic, arctic, tidal, naval, and oral)* As necessary, discuss whether each noun is a person, place, thing, or idea; for the adjectives, ask students to suggest nouns each adjective might describe.

Practice Page 15F

Review:
The unaccented ending *-al* says /əl/ as in the word *final.*

- Introduce the **Accent Patterns** for words with *-al* endings.
  SAY: In two-syllable words with the *-al* ending, accent the first syllable. In three-syllable words, accent the first syllable. If that doesn't make a recognizable word, shift the accent to the second syllable.
- Display the word *moral*, read it aloud, and point out that it is a two-syllable word that ends in *-al*. Have students point out the unaccented syllable *(al)* and the accented first syllable *(mor)*.
- Write *moral* as shown below, with a box around the accented syllable.

  [mor] al

- Then display the word *reversal*, read it aloud, and have students tell you how many syllables it has. *(three)* Ask students to tell you whether the first or second syllable is accented. *(the second syllable* ver)
- Ask a volunteer to write the word syllable by syllable and box the accented syllable.

  re [ver] sal

  If students need additional practice before working independently, follow this same procedure with other examples from the page.
- Have students read independently or with you the boxed text on 15F. Then have them complete the page, making sure they understand the directions. You may wish to suggest to students that they mark the accented syllables in the word bank before writing the words under the headings.

DIFFERENTIATING INSTRUCTION Challenge pairs of students to discuss the similar pronunciations and different meanings of the following homonym pairs: **naval**/navel, **tidal**/title, **pedal**/petal, **coral**/choral, and **metal**/medal. (The words in boldface are List 15 words.) Ask students to demonstrate understanding by using the words in sentences. Have them use a dictionary to clarify meanings. Then ask students to identify two additional ways to spell /əl/ at the end of words. *(-le, -el)*

Practice Page 15G

Review:
The unaccented ending *-ic* says /ĭk/ as in *picnic*.

- Discuss **Accent Patterns** for words with *-ic* endings.
  SAY: In words with *-ic* endings, the accent is always on the syllable just before the *-ic* ending, no matter how many syllables are in the word.
- Display the words *pathetic* and *mystic,* and have students read the words aloud with you. Ask them which syllable is accented in each word. *(the second syllable* thet; *the first syllable* mys)
- Have volunteers write each word syllable by syllable and draw a box around the accented syllable as shown below. Emphasize that even though the words have a different number of syllables, the accented syllable is always just before the *-ic* ending.

  pa [thet] ic   [mys] tic

- Have students read independently or with you the boxed text on 15G. Then have them complete the page, making sure they understand the directions.

Practice Pages 15H–15I

Review:

Nouns are words that refer to people, places, things, or ideas *(child, bedroom, car, perfection).*

Adjectives are words that describe nouns *(lively, pretty, large, swift).*

- Display the words *hero* and *heroic* as shown below, and have students read them aloud with you.

  he´ ro ⟶ he ro´ ic

- Explain that when the *-ic* ending is added to a noun, the noun becomes an adjective and the accent pattern changes: *hero* becomes *heroic*. The accent moves to the syllable just before the *-ic* ending.
- Tell students that the *-al* ending can also change a noun into an adjective.
  SAY: When the *-al* ending is added to a noun and makes it an adjective, the accent pattern changes depending on the number of syllables in the adjective.
  1. In two-syllable words with *-al* endings, the accent stays on the first syllable.
  2. In words with three or more syllables, accent the first syllable. If that doesn't make a recognizable word, keep shifting the accent to the next syllable until it makes a word you recognize.
- Display the words *coast* and *coastal,* and have students read them aloud with you. Explain that *coast* is a noun and *coastal* is an adjective. Divide *coastal* into syllables, and ask students which of the two syllables is accented. *(coast)* If students need additional practice before working independently, follow this same procedure with other examples from the page.
- Have students read independently or with you the boxed text on 15H and 15I. Then have them complete these pages, making sure they understand the directions for each activity. As needed, help students identify the accented syllable in each noun before they identify the accented syllable in each adjective.

DIFFERENTIATING INSTRUCTION Some students may need additional practice understanding and reading noun/adjective word pairs. Select a number of List 15 words that are adjectives, such as *global, natural, skeptical, universal, angelic, athletic, democratic, patriotic,* and *sarcastic.* Work with students to identify the noun forms of each word. Then have students read the noun/adjective pair, focusing on how the accent pattern is the same or different.

Spelling

OBJECTIVE *Students will spell list words with special attention to parts of speech.*

Practice Pages 15J–15K

- Have students complete 15J and 15K, making sure they understand the directions for each activity. If students need help with the activity on 15J, guide them to look for the noun in italics and complete the sentence with the adjective form of that noun.

- For the Proofreading Practice activity on 15K, explain that some of the List 15 words are spelled correctly. Tell students they should look for the two misspelled List 15 words in each sentence and correct them.

STEP 4 Work with Words in Context

Comprehension

OBJECTIVE *Students will pair list words with definitions. They will complete sentences using list words and work with parts of speech.*

Practice Pages 15L–15N

- Have students complete 15L, 15M, and 15N, making sure they understand the directions. Have them use a dictionary or work with a partner as necessary.
- For Activity 1 on 15M, review adjectives and nouns. Then display the sentence below, and guide students to identify the adjective *(allergic)* and the noun that the adjective describes *(Matt).*

Matt is allergic to dogs.

Reading, Spelling, and Writing

OBJECTIVE *Students will read and spell sentences that contain List 15 words and correctly use and spell list words.*

Practice Page 15O

- Have students complete Activities 1–3, making sure they understand the directions.

DIFFERENTIATING INSTRUCTION For students who need fluency practice, ask them to read the sentences in Activity 1 on 15O silently after they have circled the words. Then have them improve their fluency by reading the sentences aloud to a partner several times.

- For Activity 2 on 15O, choose three sentences from the first activity to dictate. Have students write the sentences on a separate piece of paper.
- For Activity 3 on 15O, challenge students to use ten List 15 words in a brief narrative or descriptive paragraph. Encourage them to be creative.

STEP 5 Monitor Progress to Increase Reading and Spelling Accuracy

Reading and Spelling Skill Check

OBJECTIVE *Students will read words from List 15 with 90 percent accuracy and record their progress on the Accuracy Checklists. Students will spell ten words from List 15 with 90 percent accuracy and record their progress on the Accuracy Checklists.*

- The fourth activity on 15O is a reading and spelling skill check.

- For each student, make two copies of **List 15/Reading Skill Check, Form A or B** (page 100). (You may also select ten words of your choice.) Give a copy to the student and ask him or her to read the words aloud to you as you indicate errors and omissions on the second copy. Share the student's performance with him or her, and have the student record the performance on the **Accuracy Checklist.**
- Provide students with a copy of the **Spelling Skill Check** (page 112). Select ten words from the list or dictate the words below. Share students' performance with them, and have students record their performance on the **Accuracy Checklist.**
  DICTATION: 1. garlic; 2. hospital; 3. public; 4. original; 5. internal; 6. plastic; 7. actual; 8. criminal; 9. picnic; 10. arctic

ASSESSMENT If students do not achieve 90 percent accuracy, or if reading and/or spelling accuracy are not improving, more practice should be done on the learning steps. Error analysis can help pinpoint the areas of concern. Skill checks should be repeated until students have achieved 90 percent accuracy or better.

STEP 6 Monitor Progress to Build Reading Proficiency

Word Proficiency

OBJECTIVE *Students will read list words with speed and accuracy.*

- The fifth activity on 15O is a word proficiency assessment.
- Once students have demonstrated that they can read a selection of List 15 words untimed with 90 percent accuracy, they should work on increasing reading speed by doing frequent rate timings.
- Use a stopwatch or second hand to time each student as he or she reads the list for a minute. A warm-up timing can be used for practice before doing a second "official" timing. If the student finishes the list in less than a minute, he or she should return to the beginning and continue to read until time is up.
- Have students record performance on the **Word Proficiency Graph**, indicating the number of words read correctly in a minute as well as the number of errors. A goal of 45 to 50 words per minute with two or fewer errors on two of three consecutive days is realistic for most students; however, goals should be individualized as appropriate.

ASSESSMENT If a student makes more than four errors on timed readings, discontinue timing the student and focus your instruction instead on reading accuracy. Identify and analyze errors and concentrate your teaching on the specific problem areas. If errors are minimal but the student is still not meeting projected goals, he or she probably needs more practice with the words. Marked improvement can often be made if the word list is practiced at home.

Passage Comprehension and Fluency

OBJECTIVE *Students will read a passage with accuracy and at a reasonable rate, with attention to expression and phrasing, and then answer vocabulary and comprehension questions about it. Students will do repeated readings of that passage to build fluency.*

Practice Page 15P

James Forten • 190 words

Passage Comprehension

- Have students look at Activity 1. Tell them they are going to read a passage that includes several List 15 words.
- Direct students to the words at the top of the page. Have students practice List 15 Words and Review Words by reading them aloud. Introduce Passage Words by reading them aloud, and give students time to read them with accuracy. Review meanings of words as necessary.
- Have students read the passage and answer the questions independently.
- For students who need additional help, provide support as necessary by identifying unknown words or pointing out the part of the passage where an answer can be found.

Fluency

- Students will be evaluated for fluency individually.
- Tell students that for Activity 2, they will be doing repeated readings of the passage to build speed and accuracy.
- Discuss fluency achievement and goals, and have students continue repeated readings until those goals are met. Between timings, have students look over the passage, reread it, and practice any words that caused difficulty.
- If students are being timed for Word Count Per Minute (WCPM), use the **Recording Form for Practice Page 15P** (page 101) to indicate any errors and to determine rate (mark number of words read by student in one minute, minus errors). Note expression and phrasing as appropriate.
- Share WCPM performance and have students record it on the **Fluency Graph.** WCPM goals should be individualized as appropriate according to grade-specific guidelines for oral reading fluency. You may wish to refer to WCPM rates of Hasbrouck and Tindal oral reading fluency data (2005).

WORD LIST 16 -*it*, -*ite*, -*et*, and -*ate* Endings

-it = /ĭt/ or /ət/	*-et* = /ĭt/ or /ət/	*-ite* = /ĭt/ or /ət/	*-ate* = /ĭt/ or /ət/	*-ate* = /āt/
audit	banquet	composite	accurate	abdicate
benefit*	basket*	definite*	affectionate	accelerate
biscuit	Bridget	exquisite	agate	accumulate
credit*	bucket	favorite*	certificate	candidate*
debit	budget	granite	chocolate*	compensate
deposit*	closet	hypocrite	climate*	concentrate
explicit	cricket	indefinite	confederate	congratulate*
habit*	diet*	opposite*	delicate	donate
implicit	fidget	prerequisite	desperate	escalate
inhabit	gadget	requisite	fortunate*	evaporate
inherit	jacket	respite	illiterate	illustrate
inhibit	market*		immaculate	isolate
limit*	planet*		immediate*	liberate
orbit	pocket		literate	ornate
profit	poet		obstinate	precipitate
prohibit*	prophet		pirate	stimulate
unit*	quiet*		private*	tolerate
	racket		senate*	vaccinate
	rocket	**-ate = /ĭt/ or /āt/**		validate
	target*			violate
	toilet	advocate		
	trumpet	appropriate		
	velvet	approximate		
	violet	delegate		
	wallet*	deliberate		
		elaborate		
		estimate*		
		graduate		
		moderate		
		separate*		

Notes:

- Suggestions for practical spelling words are indicated with an asterisk (*). Or you may want to decide with students which words they will be responsible for spelling, and have them place an asterisk next to each of those words.
- The endings *-it, -et, -ite,* and *-ate* can be pronounced /ĭt/ or /ət/. This lesson uses /ĭt/, but either pronunciation is correct.
- Some *-ate* words can be pronounced /ĭt/ or /āt/, depending on whether they are used as verbs, adjectives, or nouns.

WORD LIST 16 *-it, -ite, -et,* and *-ate* Endings

CONCEPTS COVERED

- *-it* Ending
- *-et* Ending
- *-ite* Ending
- *-ate* Ending
- Accent Patterns (REV)
- Primary Accent and Secondary Accent

As needed, review with students the **Summary of Accent Patterns** (pages 114–115; Student Book pages 101–102) before beginning instruction.

STEP 1 Work with One-Syllable Words and Word Parts

Reading and Spelling

OBJECTIVE *Students will correctly pronounce and spell the* -it, -et, -ite, *and* -ate *endings.*

Practice Page 16A

- Display the *-it, -et, -ite,* and *-ate* endings
- Remind students that in single-syllable words, the endings *-it* and *-et* have short-vowel sounds, and the endings *-ite* and *-ate* have long-vowel sounds.
- Then explain that in multisyllabic words, the ***-it, -et, -ite,*** and ***-ate* Endings** are usually pronounced /ĭt/, and they are always unaccented. Provide examples such as *quiet* and *opposite*.
- Draw attention to the ***-ate* Ending**. Tell students that in some multisyllabic words, the ending *-ate* can also say /āt/, as in *donate*.
- Display the final syllables *dit, ket, site,* and *rate,* and read them aloud with students to practice the /ĭt/ and /āt/ pronunciations.
- Have students read independently or with you the boxed text on 16A. Then have them complete the page, making sure they understand the directions for each activity.

DIFFERENTIATING INSTRUCTION For students who need further practice with the *-it, -et, -ite,* and *-ate* endings, have them make drill cards. Tell students to write each List 16 ending on an index card. They can then test one another on pronouncing the endings.

STEP 2 Work with Combined Word Parts

Reading

OBJECTIVE *Students will pronounce individual syllables and combine them to read a whole word.*

Practice Page 16B

- Display the words *favorite, accurate, deposit,* and *planet*. Have volunteers circle the *-it, -ite, -ate,* or *-et* endings. Tell them to pronounce each ending as they circle it. *(/ĭt/)* Then display the words syllable by syllable, and tell students to say the syllables to read the whole words.
- Remind students that the *-ate* ending can be pronounced in two different ways, /ĭt/ or /āt/, depending on the part of speech. Display the word *separate,* syllable by syllable, and read it twice with students, using both pronunciations. Provide context for each pronunciation; e.g., *The boys had separate lives at school* (adjective) vs. *She had to separate the boys because they were fighting* (verb).
- Note that the different pronunciations of words ending in *-ate* are covered in more detail on later Practice Pages. As necessary, explain that when an *-ate* word is used as a noun or an adjective, the ending will say /ĭt/; when an *-ate* word is used as a verb, the ending will say /āt/. Some words can be used as both nouns and adjectives.
- Have students complete 16B, making sure they understand the directions.

Practice Pages 16C–16D

- Tell students that they will be applying **Accent Patterns** to read List 16 words.

Review:
In two- and three-syllable words, accent the first syllable and pronounce it according to its syllable type. If that doesn't make a recognizable word, accent the second syllable, and pronounce the second vowel according to its syllable type.

- Display the examples below. Have volunteers draw a box around the accented syllables and read the words aloud.

  [qui] et   de [pos] it

- Tell students that in four-syllable words, the accent is usually on the second syllable. Display the example below. Have a volunteer draw a box around the accented syllable and read the word aloud.

  ap [pro] pri ate

- Have students read independently or with you the boxed text on 16D. Then have them complete 16C and 16D, making sure they understand the directions.
- **VOCABULARY** As students read and write the whole words on 16C and 16D, review selected word meanings that they may find difficult. Use the following as models.
  — A *hypocrite* is someone who gives the false appearance of having admirable beliefs or feelings.
  — An *elaborate* plan is detailed and complex; to *elaborate* is to provide greater detail about something that has been described in a broad or unclear way.

Practice Page 16E

- Tell students that in three- and four-syllable words where *-ate* is pronounced /āt/, two of the syllables will be accented.
- Then display this example:

  pre cip′ i tate′

- Explain that the first or second syllable of words in which *-ate* says /āt/ will have a **Primary Accent,** the strongest accent. The final syllable, the *-ate* ending, has a **Secondary Accent.** A secondary accent is not as strong as a primary accent, but it is stronger than no accent at all.
- Read aloud the word *precipitate* with students. Guide them to identify the syllable with the primary accent *(cip)* and the secondary accent *(tate).*
- Have students read independently or with you the boxed text on 16E. Then have them complete the page, making sure they understand the directions.

Review:
In three- and four-syllable words where *-ate* is pronounced /āt/, the primary accent is on the first or second syllable and the secondary accent is on the final syllable.

Spelling

OBJECTIVE *Students will isolate, pronounce, and spell syllables that are parts of list words. They will build vocabulary.*

Practice Page 16F

- Tell students that the *-ite* and *-ate* endings commonly spell /ĭt/ at the end of three- and four-syllable words.
- Display the following examples, and have volunteers add the correct /ĭt/ ending to make each real word. Have other students confirm the correct answers.

  fa vor ___ for tu n___

- Have students read independently or with you the boxed text on 16F. Then have them complete the page, making sure they understand the directions for each activity.

Practice Page 16G

- For Activity 1, dictate the following words. Make sure students say each word, isolate the missing syllable(s), and say the whole word as they write it.
  DICTATION: 1. pirate; 2. private; 3. poet; 4. prohibit; 5. favorite; 6. chocolate; 7. certificate; 8. definite; 9. illustrate; 10. escalate; 11. opposite; 12. inhabit; 13. inherit; 14. delicate; 15. accumulate
- Then remind students that homonyms are words that sound the same but have different spellings and meanings. Discuss the spelling and meaning of the List 16 homonyms *profit* and *prophet,* and ask volunteers to suggest sentences that reflect each meaning.
- Have students read independently or with you the boxed text on 16G. Then have them complete Activity 2, making sure they understand the directions.

STEP 3

Work with the Whole Word

Reading

OBJECTIVE *Students will apply accent patterns to read list words correctly.*

Practice Pages 16H–16I

- As needed, review accent patterns for two-, three-, and four-syllable words.
- Display the words *poet, concentrate,* and *indefinite*. Read the words aloud with students, having them listen for the accented syllables in each. Guide volunteers to write each word syllable by syllable and draw a box around the accented syllable as shown below.

  [po] et [con] cen trate in [def] i nite
- Have students complete 16H and 16I, making sure they understand the directions for each activity. For 16H, you may wish to suggest to students that they mark the accented syllables in the word bank before writing the words under the headings.
- **VOCABULARY** As students read the whole words on 16H and 16I, review selected word meanings that they may find difficult. Use the following as models.
  - — To *prohibit* is to forbid by a law or a rule.
  - — A *deliberate* act is done intentionally or on purpose; to *deliberate* is to discuss something carefully and in detail.

Review:
In two- and three-syllable words, the accent is usually on the first syllable.
In four-syllable words, the accent is usually on the second syllable.

Practice Page 16J

- Remind students that the ending *-ate* never has the primary accent.
  SAY: When the ending *-ate* says /ĭt/, it is unaccented, as in the words *climate* and *fortunate*. When the ending *-ate* says /āt/, it has a slight secondary accent, as in the word *violate*.
- Have students read independently or with you the boxed text on 16J. Then have them complete the page, making sure they understand the directions.
- Once students have sorted the words in Activity 1, have them read aloud the words in each column, paying close attention to accent patterns and the pronunciation of *-ate*.

Spelling

OBJECTIVE *Students will spell list words.*

Practice Page 16K

- Have students tell you the four different ways to spell /ĭt/ at the end of a word. *(-it, -ite, -et,* and *-ate)*
- Tell students they will be sorting some List 16 words according to spelling. Then have students complete 16K, making sure they understand the directions for each activity.

DIFFERENTIATING INSTRUCTION Provide opportunities for students to practice choosing the correct spelling for /ĭt/ at the end of words. Have partners make cards for each ending, *-it, -ite, -et,* and *-ate*. Tell one partner to say a List 16 word. Have the other partner repeat the word, hold up the card with the correct ending, and write the word. Partners can alternate roles.

STEP 4 Work with Words in Context

Comprehension

OBJECTIVE *Students will pair list words with definitions. They will complete sentences using list words and work with parts of speech.*

Practice Pages 16L–16M

- Have students complete 16L and 16M, making sure they understand the directions for each activity. Tell students to use a dictionary or work with a partner as needed.
- If students need practice dividing words into syllables before completing Activity 2 on 16L, display the words *fidget* and *certificate,* and work with them to divide each word into syllables, identify the accented syllable, and read the word aloud.

Practice Page 16N

- Remind students that the ending *-ate* can be pronounced two different ways, depending on whether the word is a noun, a verb, or an adjective. Explain that when the word is used as a noun or an adjective, the ending says /ĭt/; but when the word is used as a verb, the ending will say /āt/.
- Display the words *deliberate, advocate, approximate, moderate,* and *appropriate,* and discuss the different pronunciations, parts of speech, and meanings of each.
- Have students read independently or with you the boxed text at the top of 16N. Then have them complete the activities, making sure they understand the directions. Students may use a dictionary or work with a partner as needed.

DIFFERENTIATING INSTRUCTION For students who are having difficulty deciding when *-ate* is pronounced /ĭt/ and when it is pronounced /āt/, provide sentences similar to those below. Guide students to identify that all of the verbs say /āt/ while the nouns and adjectives say /ĭt/.

1. Mel will *graduate* in June. She will be a high school *graduate.*
2. Please *separate* the bottles from the cans. We recycle them in *separate* containers.
3. I asked the mechanic to *estimate* the cost for repairing my car. I hope that his *estimate* is not too high.
4. Brett said he had an *elaborate* plan to make money. When I asked for details, he would not *elaborate.*
5. The *delegate* was lazy. He would *delegate* all his tasks to other people.

Practice Pages 16O–16P

Review:
Adjectives are words that describe nouns (people, places, or things).

- Then ask volunteers to define *nouns* (words that name people, places, or things) and verbs (words that show action). Have students suggest several examples of nouns, adjectives, and verbs from List 16.
- Have students complete 16O and 16P, making sure they understand the directions for each activity. Have them use a dictionary or work with a partner as necessary.
- For Activity 1 on 16P, you may wish to remind students that the subject of a sentence is the person or thing performing the action in the sentence.

Practice Pages 16Q–16R

- Explain that some adjectives can be changed into nouns by using a different ending. Display the example below to demonstrate that by dropping the *-ate* and adding *-acy,* the adjective *literate* is changed to the noun *literacy.*

  liter~~ate~~ ⟶ liter + acy = literacy

- Have students read independently or with you the boxed text on 16Q. Then have them complete 16Q and 16R, making sure they understand the directions for each activity. Have them use a dictionary or work with a partner as necessary.

Reading, Spelling, and Writing

OBJECTIVE *Students will read and spell sentences that contain List 16 words and correctly use and spell list words.*

Practice Page 16S

- Have students complete Activities 1–3, making sure they understand the directions.

DIFFERENTIATING INSTRUCTION For students who need fluency practice, ask them to read the sentences in Activity 1 on 16S silently after they have circled the words. Then have them improve their fluency by reading the sentences aloud to a partner several times.

- For Activity 2 on 16S, choose three sentences from the first activity to dictate. Have students write the sentences on a separate piece of paper.
- For Activity 3 on 16S, challenge students to use ten List 16 words in a brief narrative or descriptive paragraph. Encourage them to be creative.

STEP 5 Monitor Progress to Increase Reading and Spelling Accuracy

Reading and Spelling Skill Check

OBJECTIVE *Students will read words from List 16 with 90 percent accuracy and record their progress on the Accuracy Checklists. Students will spell ten words from List 16 with 90 percent accuracy and record their progress on the Accuracy Checklists.*

- The fourth activity on 16S is a reading and spelling skill check.
- For each student, make two copies of **List 16/Reading Skill Check, Form A or B** (page 102). (You may also select ten words of your choice.) Give a copy to the student and ask him or her to read the words aloud to you as you indicate errors and omissions on the second copy. Share the student's performance with him or her, and have the student record the performance on the **Accuracy Checklist.**
- Provide students with a copy of the **Spelling Skill Check** (page 112). Select ten words from the list or dictate the words below. Share students' performance with them, and have students record their performance on the **Accuracy Checklist.**
  DICTATION: 1. fortunate; 2. estimate; 3. benefit; 4. favorite; 5. basket; 6. prohibit; 7. unit; 8. immediate; 9. candidate; 10. quiet

ASSESSMENT If students do not achieve 90 percent accuracy, or if reading and/or spelling accuracy are not improving, more practice should be done on the learning steps. Error analysis can help pinpoint the areas of concern. Skill checks should be repeated until students have achieved 90 percent accuracy or better.

STEP 6 Monitor Progress to Build Reading Proficiency

Word Proficiency

OBJECTIVE *Students will read list words with speed and accuracy.*

- The fifth activity on 16S is a word proficiency assessment.
- Once students have demonstrated that they can read a selection of List 16 words untimed with 90 percent accuracy, they should work on increasing reading speed by doing frequent rate timings.
- Use a stopwatch or second hand to time each student as he or she reads the list for a minute. A warm-up timing can be used for practice before doing a second "official" timing. If the student finishes the list in less than a minute, he or she should return to the beginning and continue to read until time is up.
- Have students record performance on the **Word Proficiency Graph**, indicating the number of words read correctly in a minute as well as the number of errors. A goal of 45 to 50 words per minute with two or fewer errors on two of three consecutive days is realistic for most students; however, goals should be individualized as appropriate.

ASSESSMENT If a student makes more than four errors on timed readings, discontinue timing the student and focus your instruction instead on reading accuracy. Identify and analyze errors and concentrate your teaching on the specific problem areas. If errors are minimal but the student is still not meeting projected goals, he or she probably needs more practice with the words. Marked improvement can often be made if the word list is practiced at home.

Passage Comprehension and Fluency

OBJECTIVE *Students will read a passage with accuracy and at a reasonable rate, with attention to expression and phrasing, and then answer vocabulary and comprehension questions about it. Students will do repeated readings of that passage to build fluency.*

Practice Page 16T

Space Firsts for American Women • 153 words

Passage Comprehension

- Have students look at Activity 1. Tell them they are going to read a passage that includes several List 16 words.
- Direct students to the words at the top of the page. Have students practice List 16 Words and Review Words by reading them aloud. Introduce Passage Words by reading them aloud, and give students time to read them with accuracy. Review meanings of words as necessary.
- Have students read the passage and answer the questions independently.
- For students who need additional help, provide support as necessary by identifying unknown words or pointing out the part of the passage where an answer can be found.

Fluency

- Students will be evaluated for fluency individually.
- Tell students that for Activity 2, they will be doing repeated readings of the passage to build speed and accuracy.
- Discuss fluency achievement and goals, and have students continue repeated readings until those goals are met. Between timings, have students look over the passage, reread it, and practice any words that caused difficulty.
- If students are being timed for Word Count Per Minute (WCPM), use the **Recording Form for Practice Page 16T** (page 103) to indicate any errors and to determine rate (mark number of words read by student in one minute, minus errors). Note expression and phrasing as appropriate.
- Share WCPM performance and have students record it on the **Fluency Graph.** WCPM goals should be individualized as appropriate according to grade-specific guidelines for oral reading fluency. You may wish to refer to WCPM rates of Hasbrouck and Tindal oral reading fluency data (2005).

WORD LIST 17 Middle-Syllable Schwa

a = /ə/	*e* = /ə/	*o* = /ə/	*u* = /ə/ or /yə/
Agatha	Adeline	abdomen	argument*
alphabet*	antelope	absolute*	calculate*
buffalo	benefit*	acrobat	incubate
Canada*	comedy	advocate	instrument
cinnamon	competent	balcony	insulate
emphasize	complement	chocolate*	insulin
escalate	congregate	Christopher	occupy*
Isabel	correlate	compromise*	pendulum
manager	delegate	custody	porcupine
matador	elephant*	customer*	regular*
Melanie	elevate	democrat	singular*
metaphor	enemy*	diplomat	stimulate
moccasin	envelope*	exodus	
ornament	execute	hypnotize	
permanent*	integrate	improvise	
pharmacist	Jeremy	innocent*	
pharmacy*	Madeline	obsolete	
relative*	persecute	octopus	
separate*	persevere	pantomime	
tentacle	remedy*	suffocate	
	segregate		
	supplement		

Note:

Suggestions for practical spelling words are indicated with an asterisk (*). Or you may want to decide with students which words they will be responsible for spelling, and have them place an asterisk next to each of those words.

WORD LIST 17 Middle-Syllable Schwa

CONCEPTS COVERED

- Middle-Syllable Schwa
- Accent Patterns (REV)

As needed, review with students the **Summary of Accent Patterns** (pages 114–115; Student Book pages 101–102) before beginning instruction.

STEP 1 Work with One-Syllable Words and Word Parts

Reading

OBJECTIVE *Students will correctly pronounce middle syllables with the schwa sound.*

Practice Page 17A

- Remind students that open syllables end in a vowel and usually have long-vowel sounds.
- Then tell students that they will be learning about open syllables in the middle of words. Introduce the **Middle-Syllable Schwa.**
  SAY: In three-syllable words, sometimes the open middle syllable is unaccented and the vowel has a schwa sound.
- Explain that there are four ways to spell the schwa sound in these middle syllables:
  1. *a* as in the syllable *ma,* pronounced /mə/ *(pharmacy)*
  2. *e* as in the syllable *te,* pronounced /tə/ *(integrate)*
  3. *o* as in the syllable *co,* pronounced /cə/ *(balcony)*
  4. *u* as in the syllable *su,* pronounced /sə/ *(insulate)*
- Display the middle syllables *ma, te, co,* and *su,* and read them aloud with students to practice the schwa sound.
- Note that the letter *u* in the middle syllable of three-syllable words can have two different sounds, /ə/ as in *insulate* and /yə/ as in *argument.* The two sounds are covered in greater detail on 17C. Also note that words with the letter *i* in the unaccented middle syllable are discussed in *Megawords 7.*
- Have students read independently or with you the boxed text on 17A. Then have them complete the page, making sure they understand the directions for each activity.

Spelling

OBJECTIVE *Students will list possible spellings for schwa syllables.*

Practice Page 17B

- Remind students that the unaccented schwa sound in the open middle syllable of List 17 words can be spelled with the vowels *a, e, o,* or *u.*
- Ask students to tell you four ways the middle syllable /trə/ might be spelled, and display the correct responses as they are given. *(tra, tre, tro, tru)* Have volunteers read the syllables aloud with the schwa sound.
- Tell students that when they spell whole words with unaccented middle syllables, they should try different vowels for the schwa sound until the word looks right.
- Have students read independently or with you the boxed text at the top of 17B. Then have them complete the page, making sure they understand the directions for each activity. For Activity 2, dictate the following syllables, giving the examples provided. **DICTATION:** 1. /rə/ as in *acrobat;* 2. /nə/ as in *ornament;* 3. /tə/ as in *customer;* 4. /ə/ as in *elephant*

Review:
Any vowel can make the schwa sound.
In List 17, the four vowels that make the schwa sound in the middle syllable are <u>a</u>, <u>e</u>, <u>o</u>, and <u>u</u>.
A syllable with a schwa sound is <u>unaccented</u>.

STEP 2 Work with Combined Word Parts

Reading

OBJECTIVE *Students will pronounce individual syllables and combine them to read a whole word.*

Practice Page 17C

- Tell students they will be applying **Accent Patterns** to read List 17 words. They will also practice identifying the vowel that makes the schwa sound in the unaccented middle syllable of these words.
- Review with students that in most three-syllable words, the first syllable is accented.
- Display the word *antelope* with its syllables separated as shown below.

  an te lope

- Say the syllables with students, and then read the whole word. Ask a volunteer to draw a box around the accented syllable. *(an)*
- Point to the second syllable and emphasize that it is an unaccented middle syllable pronounced /tə/. Explain that the vowel *e* makes a schwa sound in this syllable.

- Have students explain why the *e* makes a schwa sound. *(The first syllable,* an, *is accented, so they know that the* te *syllable is unaccented. The vowel in an unaccented middle syllable of a three-syllable word often has a schwa sound.)*
- Remind students that the letter *u* in the middle syllable of three-syllable words can have two different sounds, /ə/ or /yə/. Display the words *instrument* and *regular* syllable by syllable, and then read them aloud. Have students tell whether the *u* in each word is pronounced /ə/ or /yə/.
- Have students read independently or with you the boxed text on 17C. Then have them complete the page, making sure they understand the directions for each activity.
- As students read and write whole words on 17C, review selected word meanings that they may find difficult. Use the following as models.
  - — *Complement* means "something that completes or perfects something else." To *complement* is to make something else complete or perfect.
  - — *Insulate* means "to cover to prevent heat loss." It also means "to protect or shield."
  - — *Insulin* is a substance that helps control blood-sugar levels, and it is often used to treat diabetes.

Spelling

OBJECTIVE *Students will isolate, pronounce, and spell syllables that are parts of list words.*

Practice Page 17D

- For Activity 1, dictate the following words. Make sure that students spell the missing syllables and say the whole word as they write it.
  DICTATION: 1. ornament; 2. elevate; 3. alphabet; 4. diplomat; 5. calculate; 6. customer; 7. benefit; 8. relative; 9. absolute; 10. instrument
- For Activity 2, dictate the following words slowly, separating the syllables and repeating the whole word. Guide students to use the headings to help them spell the middle-syllable schwa in each word. Make sure students understand that they should write the words syllable by syllable.
  DICTATION: 1. manager; 2. permanent; 3. matador; 4. Canada; 5. antelope; 6. elephant; 7. comedy; 8. envelope; 9. acrobat; 10. octopus; 11. absolute; 12. compromise; 13. porcupine; 14. argument; 15. insulin; 16. instrument
- **VOCABULARY** As students write and pronounce the words on 17D, review selected word meanings that they may find difficult. Use the following as models.
  - — *Absolute* silence is total and complete silence; an *absolute* ruler has no limits to his or her power.
  - — A *compromise* refers to a way that two or more people can reach an agreement by each giving up something.

DIFFERENTIATING INSTRUCTION For students who are ready to work with middle-syllable schwa within whole words, display a series of List 17 words with the middle vowel missing (e.g., *dem___crat, mat___dor, ins___late, com___dy),* and ask students to fill in the correct middle vowel. If necessary, have students try several different vowels before determining which one "looks right."

STEP 3

Work with the Whole Word

Reading

OBJECTIVE *Students will apply accent patterns to read list words correctly.*

Practice Page 17E

- Display the word *subjugate,* and have students explain how to divide the word into syllables. Then ask volunteers to identify the accented syllable *(sub)* and mark the vowels as shown below. If necessary, explain that they should mark the vowel in each syllable short, long, or schwa.

  sŭb jə̂u gāte

- Have students complete 17E, making sure they understand the directions. Point out that all of the words on the page are accented on the first syllable. Also note that students need not conform precisely to dictionary standards of dividing syllables, as long as their versions make sense and enable them to sound out the words correctly.

Review:
The accent in these words is on the first syllable. The middle syllable is unaccented and has a schwa sound.

Spelling

OBJECTIVE *Students will spell list words with special attention to middle-syllable schwa.*

Practice Pages 17F–17G

- Tell students that they will be doing some activities to help them remember how to spell the schwa sound in middle syllables of List 17 words.
- Display the word *innocent,* and have volunteers identify the vowel that makes the schwa sound. *(o)* Ask students which other vowels can make the schwa sound. *(a, e, u)*
- Then display these incomplete words:

  env___lope   rel___tive

- Model identifying the vowel that spells the schwa sound in *envelope;* you may wish to begin by filling in incorrect vowels before coming up with the correct answer that "looks right." Then ask a volunteer to use the same process to identify the vowel that spells the schwa sound in *relative.*
- Have students complete 17F and 17G, making sure they understand the directions.

DIFFERENTIATING INSTRUCTION For students who need reinforcement spelling words with the middle-syllable schwa, try a game. Select a number of List 17 words from 17G. Divide the words into two lists, and distribute each list to a team. Have the teams write each word from their list on a card. Then have one team read a word, and have a player on the other team say, spell, and write it. Then have the teams reverse roles. If a word is misspelled, have the team put the card aside. At the end, have teams review and practice saying, writing, and spelling misspelled words.

STEP 4 Work with Words in Context

Comprehension

OBJECTIVE *Students will pair list words with definitions. They will complete sentences using list words and work with parts of speech.*

Practice Pages 17H–17J

- Have students complete 17H, 17I, and 17J, making sure they understand the directions for each activity. For 17I, point out that they will need to fill in more than one word for some sentences. Have students use a dictionary or work with a partner as necessary.

Practice Pages 17K–17M

Review:
Verbs are words that show actions.
Nouns are words that refer to people, places, things, or ideas.
Adjectives are words that describe people, places, things, or ideas.

- Have students complete 17K, 17L, and 17M, making sure they understand the directions. Have them use a dictionary or work with a partner as necessary.

Reading, Spelling, and Writing

OBJECTIVE *Students will read and spell sentences that contain List 17 words and correctly use and spell list words.*

Practice Page 17N

- Have students complete Activities 1–3, making sure they understand the directions.

DIFFERENTIATING INSTRUCTION For students who need fluency practice, ask them to read the sentences in Activity 1 on 17N silently after they have circled the words. Then have them improve their fluency by reading the sentences aloud to a partner several times.

- For Activity 2 on 17N, choose three sentences from the first activity to dictate. Have students write the sentences on a separate piece of paper.
- For Activity 3 on 17N, challenge students to use ten List 17 words in a brief narrative or descriptive paragraph. Encourage them to be creative.

STEP 5 Monitor Progress to Increase Reading and Spelling Accuracy

Reading and Spelling Skill Check

OBJECTIVE *Students will read words from List 17 with 90 percent accuracy and record their progress on the Accuracy Checklists. Students will spell ten words from List 17 with 90 percent accuracy and record their progress on the Accuracy Checklists.*

- The fourth activity on 17N is a reading and spelling skill check.
- For each student, make two copies of **List 17/Reading Skill Check, Form A or B** (page 104). (You may also select ten words of your choice.) Give a copy to the student and ask him or her to read the words aloud to you as you indicate errors and omissions on the second copy. Share the student's performance with him or her, and have the student record the performance on the **Accuracy Checklist.**
- Provide students with a copy of the **Spelling Skill Check** (page 112). Select ten words from the list or dictate the words below. Share students' performance with them, and have students record their performance on the **Accuracy Checklist.**
  DICTATION: 1. manager; 2. separate; 3. absolute; 4. elevate; 5. integrate; 6. permanent; 7. argument; 8. enemy; 9. compromise; 10. regular

ASSESSMENT If students do not achieve 90 percent accuracy, or if reading and/or spelling accuracy are not improving, more practice should be done on the learning steps. Error analysis can help pinpoint the areas of concern. Skill checks should be repeated until students have achieved 90 percent accuracy or better.

STEP 6 Monitor Progress to Build Reading Proficiency

Word Proficiency

OBJECTIVE *Students will read list words with speed and accuracy.*

- The fifth activity on 17N is a word proficiency assessment.
- Once students have demonstrated that they can read a selection of List 17 words untimed with 90 percent accuracy, they should work on increasing reading speed by doing frequent rate timings.
- Use a stopwatch or second hand to time each student as he or she reads the list for a minute. A warm-up timing can be used for practice before doing a second "official" timing. If the student finishes the list in less than a minute, he or she should return to the beginning and continue to read until time is up.
- Have students record performance on the **Word Proficiency Graph,** indicating the number of words read correctly in a minute as well as the number of errors. A goal of 45 to 50 words per minute with two or fewer errors on two of three consecutive days is realistic for most students; however, goals should be individualized as appropriate.

ASSESSMENT If a student makes more than four errors on timed readings, discontinue timing the student and focus your instruction instead on reading accuracy. Identify and analyze errors and concentrate your teaching on the specific problem areas. If errors are minimal but the student is still not meeting projected goals, he or she probably needs more practice with the words. Marked improvement can often be made if the word list is practiced at home.

Passage Comprehension and Fluency

OBJECTIVE *Students will read a passage with accuracy and at a reasonable rate, with attention to expression and phrasing, and then answer vocabulary and comprehension questions about it. Students will do repeated readings of that passage to build fluency.*

Practice Page 170

A Smart Invertebrate? • 155 words

Passage Comprehension

- Have students look at Activity 1. Tell them they are going to read a passage that includes several List 17 words.
- Direct students to the words at the top of the page. Have students practice List 17 Words and Review Words by reading them aloud. Introduce Passage Words by reading them aloud, and give students time to read them with accuracy. Review meanings of words as necessary.
- Have students read the passage and answer the questions independently.
- For students who need additional help, provide support as necessary by identifying unknown words or pointing out the part of the passage where an answer can be found.

Fluency

- Students will be evaluated for fluency individually.
- Tell students that for Activity 2, they will be doing repeated readings of the passage to build speed and accuracy.
- Discuss fluency achievement and goals, and have students continue repeated readings until those goals are met. Between timings, have students look over the passage, reread it, and practice any words that caused difficulty.
- If students are being timed for Word Count Per Minute (WCPM), use the **Recording Form for Practice Page 170** (page 105) to indicate any errors and to determine rate (mark number of words read by student in one minute, minus errors). Note expression and phrasing as appropriate.
- Share WCPM performance and have students record it on the **Fluency Graph.** WCPM goals should be individualized as appropriate according to grade-specific guidelines for oral reading fluency. You may wish to refer to WCPM rates of Hasbrouck and Tindal oral reading fluency data (2005).

REVIEW LIST 15–17

abdomen
absolute*
accidental
affectionate
allergic
alphabet*
argument*
athletic*
balcony
benefit*
biscuit
budget
central*
climate*
compromise*
customer*
deliberate
donate
electric*
emphasize
enemy*
energetic
favorite*
habit*
heroic
immediate*
indefinite
instrument
legal*
manager
music*
national*
original*
planet*
plural
private*
public*
regular
remedy*
separate*
trial*
wallet*

Note:

Words suggested as practical spelling words in Lists 15–17 are indicated with an asterisk (*).

REVIEW LIST 15–17

Review Pages 55–58

- Have students read independently or with you the Review List on page 55.
- Review the endings and syllables covered in Lists 15–17 as necessary. Then have students complete pages 56–58, making sure they understand the directions.
- For Activities 4 and 6, have students work with a partner or use the dictionary.

STEP 5 Monitor Progress to Increase Reading and Spelling Accuracy

Reading and Spelling Skill Check

OBJECTIVE *Students will read and spell words from Review List: 15–17 with 90 percent accuracy and record their progress on the Accuracy Checklists.*

- For each student, make two copies of **Review List: 15–17/Reading Assessment, Form A or B** (page 106). (You may also select ten words of your choice.) Ask the student to read the words aloud as you indicate errors and omissions. Share the student's performance, and have the student record it on the **Accuracy Checklist.**
- Provide students with a copy of the **Spelling Assessment** (page 112). Select ten words from the list or dictate the words below. Share students' performance with them, and have students record their performance on the **Accuracy Checklist.**
  DICTATION: 1. athletic; 2. emphasize; 3. favorite; 4. trial; 5. heroic; 6. regular; 7. instrument; 8. electric; 9. national; 10. energetic

ASSESSMENT Skill checks should be repeated until students have achieved 90 percent accuracy or better.

STEP 6 Monitor Progress to Build Reading Proficiency

Word Proficiency

OBJECTIVE *Students will read list words with speed and accuracy.*

- Once students have demonstrated that they can read a selection of review list words untimed with 90 percent accuracy, they should work on increasing reading speed.
- Use a stopwatch or second hand to time each student as he or she reads the list for a minute. A warm-up timing can be used for practice. If the student finishes the list in less than a minute, he or she should return to the beginning and continue to read.
- Have students record performance on the **Word Proficiency Graph,** indicating the number of words read correctly in a minute as well as the number of errors.

ASSESSMENT If a student makes more than four errors on timed readings, discontinue the timing and focus on reading accuracy. Identify and analyze errors and concentrate on problem areas.

WORD LIST 18 -ant, -ance, -ent, and -ence Endings

-ant = /ənt/

abundant
applicant
arrogant
assailant
assistant*
attendant
compliant
constant
defendant
defiant
distant*
dominant
elegant
fragrant
hesitant
ignorant*
important*
infant*
inhabitant
instant
malignant
occupant
pleasant*
pregnant
resistant
servant
significant*
tolerant
truant
vacant

-ance = /əns/

abundance
acceptance*
ambulance
appearance*
appliance*
arrogance
assistance
attendance*
balance*
clearance
compliance
defiance
distance*
dominance
elegance
endurance
entrance*
fragrance
hindrance
ignorance
importance*
instance
insurance*
perseverance
relevance
resistance
significance
substance
tolerance

-ent = /ənt/

absent*
adjacent
affluent
agent*
client
competent
confident*
consistent*
correspondent
decent
delinquent
dependent
different*
evident
excellent*
frequent*
independent*
innocent*
intelligent*
magnificent
negligent
obedient
present*
president*
recent*
resident
reverent
silent*
student
violent*

-ence = /əns/

absence
affluence
audience*
competence
confidence*
correspondence
dependence*
difference*
essence
evidence*
excellence
experience*
independence
influence*
innocence
intelligence
magnificence
negligence
obedience
preference
presence
residence
reverence
science*
silence*
violence*

-ancy = /ancy/

hesitancy
infancy
malignancy
occupancy
pregnancy
truancy
vacancy*

-ency = /əncy/

agency*
competency
consistency
decency
delinquency
frequency
presidency
residency

Note:

Suggestions for practical spelling words are indicated with an asterisk (*). Or you may want to decide with students which words they will be responsible for spelling, and have them place an asterisk next to each of those words.

WORD LIST 18 *-ant, -ance, -ent,* and *-ence* Endings

CONCEPTS COVERED

- *-ant* Ending
- *-ance* Ending
- *-ent* Ending
- *-ence* Ending
- Accent Patterns (REV)

As needed, review with students the **Summary of Accent Patterns** (pages 114–115; Student Book pages 101–102) before beginning instruction.

STEP 1 Work with One-Syllable Words and Word Parts

Reading and Spelling

OBJECTIVE *Students will correctly pronounce and spell the* -ant, -ance, -ent, *and* -ence *endings.*

Practice Page 18A

- Display the *-ant, -ent, -ance,* and *-ence* endings.
- Remind students that in single-syllable words, the endings *-ant, -ent, -ance,* and *-ence* have short-vowel sounds.
- Explain that these endings sound different in multisyllabic words. In multisyllabic words, these endings are unaccented and have the schwa sound (/ə/).
- Tell students that the ***-ant*** and ***-ent* Endings** are usually pronounced /ənt/ in multisyllabic words, as in *servant* and *present*. The ***-ance*** and ***-ence* Endings** are usually pronounced /əns/, as in *distance* and *absence*.
- Display the final syllables *vant, vance, sent,* and *sence,* and read them aloud with students to practice the /ənt/ and /əns/ pronunciations.
- Have students read independently or with you the boxed text on 18A. Then have them complete the page, making sure they understand the directions for each activity.

Practice Page 18B

- Display the words *servant, present, distance,* and *absence*. Remind students that the unaccented ending /ənt/ can be spelled either *-ant* or *-ent*. Then remind students that the unaccented ending /əns/ can be spelled either *-ance* or *-ence*.
- Ask volunteers to suggest two possible spellings for a syllable that is pronounced /bənt/. *(bent, bant)* Then ask volunteers to suggest two possible spellings for a syllable that is pronounced /fəns/. *(fence, fance)*
- Have students read independently or with you the boxed text on 18B. Then have them complete the page, making sure they understand the directions for each activity.

- Dictate the following syllables for Activity 2, giving the examples provided. Make sure that students repeat the endings while spelling them.
  DICTATION: 1. /rəns/ as in *appearance* or *difference;* 2. /dənt/ as in *dependent* or *defendant;* 3. /təns/ as in *distance* or *sentence;* 4. /rənt/ as in *ignorant* or *different;* 5. /lənt/ as in *excellent* or *stimulant;* 6. /ənt/ as in *truant* or *client;* 7. /əns/ as in *science* or *defiance;* 8. /ləns/ as in *ambulance* or *silence*

DIFFERENTIATING INSTRUCTION For students who need further practice with the pronunciation and spelling of the endings *-ant, -ance, -ent,* and *-ence,* drill cards can be helpful. Make cards with the endings *-ant, -ance, -ent,* and *-ence* on one side and the pronunciations /ənt/ or /əns/ on the other. Students can be asked to read the endings or to tell the ways a certain pronunciation can be spelled.

STEP 2 Work with Combined Word Parts

Reading

OBJECTIVE *Students will pronounce individual syllables and combine them to read a whole word.*

Practice Page 18C

- Display these examples.

dis tant	distant	dis tance	distance
va cant	vacant	va can cy	vacancy

- Point out that the endings *-ant* and *-ance* are unaccented and contain the schwa sound. Explain that the ending *-ancy* is a variation of *-ance* and is also unaccented.
- Model reading the syllables and the whole words aloud. For each word, have volunteers point out the *-ant, -ance,* and *-ancy* endings, draw a box around the accented syllable, and mark the vowel in the accented syllable long or short.
- As appropriate, discuss parts of speech. Explain that multisyllabic words ending in *-ant* are often adjectives *(distant, vacant),* while words ending in *-ance* and *-ancy* are nouns *(distance, vacancy).* Ask students to tell you what happens to the accented syllable when these words change from adjectives to nouns. *(It stays the same.)*
- Have students read independently or with you the boxed text on 18C. Then have them complete the page, making sure they understand the directions for each activity.
- **VOCABULARY** As students read the whole words on 18C, review selected word meanings that they may find difficult. Use the following as models.
  — An *arrogant* person is conceited and over-proud; such a person shows *arrogance.*
  — The words *compliant* and *resistant* (and *compliance* and *resistance)* are antonyms. If you are *compliant* with a rule, you go along with it; you show *compliance.* If you are *resistant* to a rule, you are against it; you show *resistance.*

Practice Page 18D

- Use the procedure from 18C to introduce the *-ent, -ence,* and *-ency* endings and these examples:

si lent	silent	si lence	silence
fre quent	frequent	fre quen cy	frequency

- As appropriate, discuss parts of speech. Explain that multisyllabic words ending in *-ent* are often adjectives *(silent, frequent)*, while words ending in *-ence* and *-ency* are nouns *(silence, frequency)*. Ask students to tell you what happens to the accented syllable when these words change from adjectives to nouns. *(It stays the same.)*
- Have students read independently or with you the boxed text on 18D. Then have them complete the page, making sure they understand the directions for each activity.
- **VOCABULARY** As students read the whole words on 18D, review selected word meanings that they may find difficult. Use the following as models.
  - — Someone who is *affluent* has a lot of money; *affluence* is wealth.
  - — A *correspondent* is someone who communicates in writing; a *correspondent* may also be a person who provides television or newspaper reports from a particular place. *Correspondence* is communication (often through writing).

Spelling

OBJECTIVE *Students will isolate, pronounce, and spell syllables that are parts of list words.*

Practice Page 18E

- For Activity 1, dictate the following words. Make sure students say each word, isolate the missing syllable(s), and say the whole word as they write it.
  DICTATION: 1. servant; 2. distance; 3. absent; 4. silence; 5. ignorance; 6. constant; 7. dominant; 8. important; 9. agent; 10. preference
- For Activity 2, dictate the following words. Several dictated words have unaccented *i*'s *(inhabitant, evidence, residence)* which should be pronounced with the short-*i* sound so that students spell them correctly. Overpronounce the double consonants in *different* and *excellent* so that students hear the sounds in both syllables.
  DICTATION: 1. negligence; 2. important; 3. insurance; 4. silence; 5. inhabitant; 6. different; 7. ignorance; 8. defendant; 9. excellent; 10. substance; 11. independent; 12. significant; 13. ambulance; 14. dependence; 15. resident; 16. evidence

DIFFERENTIATING INSTRUCTION Tell students that one way to learn the correct spellings for words with the endings *-ant, -ance, -ent,* and *-ence* is to create and memorize sentences that contain clues to help them recall the spellings. You may wish to explain that these mnemonic sentences are more likely to be memorable if they describe something silly or personally significant. For example:

An import*ant ant* pays a differ*ent* r*ent*.
Will you make an appear*ance* in Fr*ance?*

Have partners work together to write their own mnemonic sentences for several List 18 words. Clue words in the sentences should be familiar and easily spelled.

STEP 3

Work with the Whole Word

Reading

OBJECTIVE *Students will apply accent patterns to read list words correctly.*

Practice Page 18F

- Review **Accent Patterns**. Point out that most two- and three-syllable words are accented on the first syllable, but that three-syllable words with a prefix, root, and suffix are usually accented on the second syllable.
- Display the words *client* and *abundance* and read them aloud, telling students to listen for the accented syllable in each word. Have volunteers write each word syllable by syllable and draw a box around the accented syllable as shown below. If necessary, point out that the List 18 endings can be considered suffixes for the purposes of syllabicating three-syllable words.

  [cli] ent   a [bun] dance

- Have students complete 18F, making sure they understand the directions. You may wish to suggest to students that they mark the accented syllables in the word bank before writing the words under the headings.
- **VOCABULARY** As students read the whole words on this page, review selected word meanings that they may find difficult. Use the following as models.
  — A *truant* is someone who is absent without permission, especially from school. *Truant* can also be used to describe such a person.
  — A tumor or disease that is *malignant* may cause death unless effectively treated; *malignant* is also used to describe someone or something that is evil or hateful and showing a desire to harm others.

Spelling

OBJECTIVE *Students will spell list words with special attention to schwa endings and parts of speech.*

Practice Pages 18G–18H

- Tell students that they will be learning when to use the different List 18 endings.
- Display the examples below. Point out that when adjectives ending in *-ant* or *-ent* are are changed into nouns, the new ending will have the same vowel as the old ending. Have volunteers underline the *a* in *distant* and *distance* and the *e* in *silent* and *silence.*

  dist<u>a</u>nt ⟷ dist<u>a</u>nce   sil<u>e</u>nt ⟷ sil<u>e</u>nce

- Have students read independently or with you the boxed text at the top of 18H. Then have them complete 18G and 18H, making sure they understand the directions for each activity.

Review:
Words ending in *-ant* or *-ent* are <u>adjectives</u>.
Words ending in *-ance* or *-ence* are <u>nouns</u>.

Practice Pages 18I–18J

- Tell students that the letters *c* and *g* often show up before /ənt/ or /əns/ endings. Review with students that the letters *c* and *g* have both hard and soft sounds.
- Display the following examples:

Hard sounds:	vacant	elegance
Soft sounds:	decent	intelligence

- Read the examples with students and work with them to identify the hard sounds of *c* (/k/) and *g* (/g/) and the soft sounds of *c* (/s/) and *g* (/j/).
- Guide students to understand that when they hear a hard *c* or *g* before an /ənt/ or /əns/ ending, the ending begins with the letter *a*. Lead them to generalize that when they hear a soft *c* or *g* before an /ənt/ or /əns/ ending, the ending begins with the letter *e*.
- Have students read independently or with you the boxed text on 18I. Then have them complete 18I and 18J, making sure they understand the directions for each activity.
- As students sort the words in Activity 1 on 18I, you may wish to emphasize that they will be looking for the *c* or *g* that appears *just before* the ending. Once students have sorted the words, have them read each column aloud. Tell them to listen for the hard and soft *c* and *g* sounds as they pay close attention to the spelling of the word endings.

Practice Page 18K

- Remind students that if the adjective form of a word ends in *-ant,* the noun form ends in *-ance* or *-ancy.* Have a volunteer say the spelling of the noun form when the adjective form ends in *-ent. (-ence* or *-ency)*
- Have students read independently or with you the boxed text at the top of 18K. Then have them complete the page, making sure they understand the directions for each activity. Note that while *hesitancy* is the preferred answer for item 2, *hesitance* would also be correct.

> **DIFFERENTIATING INSTRUCTION** It may be appropriate to give some students practice working with word families. Challenge partners to list noun and adjective forms of the verbs *assist, attend, comply, prefer, confide, signify, dominate,* and *depend.* Point out that the words they list do not have to appear on List 18.

STEP 4 Work with Words in Context

Comprehension

OBJECTIVE *Students will pair list words with definitions. They will complete sentences using list words and work with parts of speech.*

Practice Pages 18L–18N

- Tell students that the endings *-ant* and *-ent* often mean "a person who..." Ask them to suggest meanings for *servant (a person who serves)* and *resident (a person who resides).*

- Display the words *entrance* and *preference*. Remind students that words that end in *-ance* or *-ence* are nouns. Point out that these words often refer to a way of doing something or the state of one who acts in a certain way. Then explain that these words often have an identifiable verb in the root, and have volunteers identify the verbs. *(enter, prefer)*
- Then explain that it can be helpful for students to associate members of a word family. Display the word *hesitancy,* and have volunteers determine the verb and adjective forms of the word. *(hesitate, hesitant)*
- Have students read independently or with you the boxed text on 18L and 18M. Then have them complete 18L, 18M, and 18N, making sure they understand the directions for each activity.

Practice Pages 18O–18P

- Have students complete 18O and 18P, making sure they understand the directions for each activity. Have them use a dictionary or work with a partner as necessary.

Reading, Spelling, and Writing

OBJECTIVE *Students will read and spell sentences that contain List 18 words and correctly use and spell list words.*

Practice Page 18Q

- Have students complete Activities 1–3, making sure they understand the directions.

> **DIFFERENTIATING INSTRUCTION** For students who need fluency practice, ask them to read the sentences in Activity 1 on 18Q silently after they have circled the words. Then have them improve their fluency by reading the sentences aloud to a partner several times.

- For Activity 2 on 18N, choose three sentences from the first activity to dictate. Have students write the sentences on a separate piece of paper.
- For Activity 3 on 18N, challenge students to use ten List 18 words in a brief narrative or descriptive paragraph. Encourage them to be creative.

STEP 5 Monitor Progress to Increase Reading and Spelling Accuracy

Reading and Spelling Skill Check

OBJECTIVE *Students will read words from List 18 with 90 percent accuracy and record their progress on the Accuracy Checklists. Students will spell ten words from List 18 with 90 percent accuracy and record their progress on the Accuracy Checklists.*

- The fourth activity on 18Q is a reading and spelling skill check.
- For each student, make two copies of **List 18/Reading Skill Check, Form A or B** (page 107). (You may also select ten words of your choice.) Give a copy to the student and ask him or her to read the words aloud to you as you indicate errors and omissions on the second copy. Share the student's performance with him or her, and have the student record the performance on the **Accuracy Checklist.**

- Provide students with a copy of the **Spelling Skill Check** (page 112). Select ten words from the list or dictate the words below. Share students' performance with them, and have students record their performance on the **Accuracy Checklist.**
  DICTATION: 1. important; 2. agency; 3. balance; 4. confident; 5. vacancy; 6. excellent; 7. science; 8. pleasant; 9. consistent; 10. experience

ASSESSMENT If students do not achieve 90 percent accuracy, or if reading and/or spelling accuracy are not improving, more practice should be done on the learning steps. Error analysis can help pinpoint the areas of concern. Skill checks should be repeated until students have achieved 90 percent accuracy or better.

STEP 6 Monitor Progress to Build Reading Proficiency

Word Proficiency

OBJECTIVE *Students will read list words with speed and accuracy.*

- The fifth activity on 18Q is a word proficiency assessment.
- Once students have demonstrated that they can read a selection of List 18 words untimed with 90 percent accuracy, they should work on increasing reading speed by doing frequent rate timings.
- Use a stopwatch or second hand to time each student as he or she reads the list for a minute. A warm-up timing can be used for practice before doing a second "official" timing. If the student finishes the list in less than a minute, he or she should return to the beginning and continue to read until time is up.
- Have students record performance on the **Word Proficiency Graph**, indicating the number of words read correctly in a minute as well as the number of errors. A goal of 45 to 50 words per minute with two or fewer errors on two of three consecutive days is realistic for most students; however, goals should be individualized as appropriate.

ASSESSMENT If a student makes more than four errors on timed readings, discontinue timing the student and focus your instruction instead on reading accuracy. Identify and analyze errors and concentrate your teaching on the specific problem areas. If errors are minimal but the student is still not meeting projected goals, he or she probably needs more practice with the words. Marked improvement can often be made if the word list is practiced at home.

Passage Comprehension and Fluency

OBJECTIVE *Students will read a passage with accuracy and at a reasonable rate, with attention to expression and phrasing, and then answer vocabulary and comprehension questions about it. Students will do repeated readings of that passage to build fluency.*

Practice Page 18R

Cutting Dependence on Oil • 157 words

Passage Comprehension

- Have students look at Activity 1. Tell them they are going to read a passage that includes several List 18 words.
- Direct students to the words at the top of the page. Have students practice List 18 Words and Review Words by reading them aloud. Introduce Passage Words by reading them aloud, and give students time to read them with accuracy. Review meanings of words as necessary.
- Have students read the passage and answer the questions independently.
- For students who need additional help, provide support as necessary by identifying unknown words or pointing out the part of the passage where an answer can be found.

Fluency

- Students will be evaluated for fluency individually.
- Tell students that for Activity 2, they will be doing repeated readings of the passage to build speed and accuracy.
- Discuss fluency achievement and goals, and have students continue repeated readings until those goals are met. Between timings, have students look over the passage, reread it, and practice any words that caused difficulty.
- If students are being timed for Word Count Per Minute (WCPM), use the **Recording Form for Practice Page 18R** (page 108) to indicate any errors and to determine rate (mark number of words read by student in one minute, minus errors). Note expression and phrasing as appropriate.
- Share WCPM performance and have students record it on the **Fluency Graph.** WCPM goals should be individualized as appropriate according to grade-specific guidelines for oral reading fluency. You may wish to refer to WCPM rates of Hasbrouck and Tindal oral reading fluency data (2005).

WORD LIST 19 *-ive, -ice, -ace, -ine,* and *-ain* Endings

-ive = /ĭv/	*-ice, -ace* = /ĭs/ or /əs/*	*-ine, -ain* = /ĭn/ or /ən/**	*-ine* = /ēn/
abusive	accomplice	bargain*	chlorine
active*	apprentice	captain	figurine
attractive	cowardice	certain*	gasoline*
captive	crevice	chaplain	machine*
creative*	furnace*	chieftain	magazine*
detective	grimace	curtain	marine
elective	justice*	determine*	mezzanine
expensive*	menace	discipline*	Pauline
fugitive	notice*	doctrine	routine*
massive	novice	engine*	sardine
motive	office*	examine*	submarine
native	practice*	famine	vaccine
negative*	preface	feminine*	
passive*	prejudice*	fountain	
perceptive	service*	genuine	
positive*	surface*	imagine*	
productive	terrace	Madeline	
relative*	Wallace	masculine*	
repulsive		medicine*	
respective		mountain*	
sensitive		porcelain	
		villain	

Notes:

- Suggestions for practical spelling words are indicated with an asterisk (*). Or you may want to decide with students which words they will be responsible for spelling, and have them place an asterisk next to each of those words.
- The endings *-ice* or *-ace* can be pronounced /ĭs/ or /əs/. This lesson uses /ĭs/, but either pronunciation is correct.
- The endings *-ine* or *-ain* can be pronounced /ĭn/ or /ən/. This lesson uses /ĭn/, but either pronunciation is correct.

WORD LIST 19 *-ive, -ice, -ace, -ine,* and *-ain* Endings

CONCEPTS COVERED

- *-ive* Ending
- *-ice* and *-ace* Endings
- *-ine* and *-ain* Endings
- Accent Patterns (REV)
- Primary Accent (REV)
- Secondary Accent (REV)

As needed, review with students the **Summary of Accent Patterns** (pages 114–115; Student Book pages 101–102) before beginning instruction.

STEP 1 Work with One-Syllable Words and Word Parts

Reading and Spelling

OBJECTIVE *Students will correctly pronounce and spell the* -ive, -ice, -ace, -ine, *and* -ain *endings.*

Practice Page 19A

- Display the *-ive, -ice, -ace, -ine,* and *-ain* endings.
- Remind students that in single-syllable words, these endings have long-vowel sounds.
- Explain that in multisyllabic words the endings *-ive, -ice, -ace, -ine,* and *-ain* usually have the same vowel sound, short *i:* the ***-ive* Ending** says /ĭv/, the ***-ice* and *-ace* Endings** say /ĭs/, and the ***-ine* and *-ain* Endings** say /ĭn/. Provide *off<u>ice</u>* and *curt<u>ain</u>* as examples.
- Draw attention to the ***-ine* Ending.** Tell students that in some multisyllabic words, the *-ine* ending can have a long-*e* sound and say /ēn/. Provide an example such as *mach<u>ine</u>.*
- Display the final syllables *tive, fice, nace, tain,* and *dine,* and read them aloud with students to practice the short-*i* (and long-*e*) vowel sounds.
- Have students read independently or with you the boxed text on 19A. Then have them complete the page, making sure they understand the directions for each activity.

Practice Page 19B

- Display the words *office* and *surface* and underline the *-ice* and *-ace* endings. **SAY:** The unaccented ending /ĭs/ can be spelled either *-ice* or *-ace* as in *office* and *surface.*
- Ask volunteers to suggest two possible spellings for a syllable that is pronounced /lĭs/. *(lice* or *lace)*
- Display the words *engine* and *curtain* and underline the *-ine* and *-ain* endings. **SAY:** The unaccented ending /ĭn/ can be spelled either *-ine* or *-ain* as in *engine* and *curtain.*
- Ask volunteers to suggest two possible spellings for a syllable that is pronounced /tĭn/. *(tine* or *tain)*

- Have students read independently or with you the boxed text on 19B. Then have them complete the page, making sure they understand the directions for each activity.

> **DIFFERENTIATING INSTRUCTION** For students who need further practice with *-ive, -ice, -ace, -ain,* and *-ine* endings, have them make drill cards. Tell students to write each List 19 ending on one side and its pronunciation(s) *(/ĭv/, /ĭs/, /ĭn/,* or */ēn/)* on the other. They can then test one another on reading and spelling the endings.

STEP 2 Work with Combined Word Parts

Reading

OBJECTIVE *Students will pronounce individual syllables and combine them to read a whole word.*

Practice Page 19C

Review:
-ice and *-ace* are unaccented endings that say /ĭs/ as in *office* and *surface.*

- Display the word *active* and underline the *-ive* ending.
  SAY: *-ive* is an unaccented ending that says /ĭv/ as in *active.*
- Explain to students that because the endings *-ice, -ace,* and *-ive* are unaccented, the accent will be on another syllable in the word.
- Display the words *office, surface,* and *active* syllable by syllable. Have volunteers draw a box around the accented syllable and read each word aloud.
  [of] fice   [sur] face   [ac] tive
- Have students read independently or with you the boxed text on 19C. Then have them complete the page, making sure they understand the directions for each activity.
- As necessary, review **Accent Patterns** with students.

Practice Page 19D

- Display the words *engine* and *curtain,* and underline the *-ine* and *-ain* endings.
  SAY: *-ine* and *-ain* are unaccented endings that that say /ĭn/ as in *engine* and *curtain.*
- Explain to students that because the *-ine* and *-ain* (/ĭn/) endings are unaccented, the accent will be on another syllable in the word.
- Display *engine* and *curtain* syllable by syllable and have volunteers draw a box around the accented syllable in each.
- Display the words *machine* and *magazine* and underline the *-ine* endings. Tell students that *-ine* also says /ēn/ as in *machine* and *magazine.*
  SAY: In two-syllable words that end with /ēn/, the final syllable has the accent. In three-syllable words that end with /ēn/, the first syllable has the **Primary Accent** and the final syllable has a **Secondary Accent**.
- Display the word *machine* syllable by syllable, and point out that it has two syllables. Ask students to say which syllable is accented. *(the second, chine)*

- Then display *magazine* syllable by syllable. Have a volunteer say how many syllables it has. *(three)* Guide students to identify that the first syllable *(mag)* has the primary accent and the final syllable *(zine)* has a secondary accent.
- Have students read independently or with you the boxed text on 19D. Then have them complete the page, making sure they understand the directions.
- **VOCABULARY** As students read and write whole words in Activities 1 and 2, review selected word meanings that they may find difficult. Use the following as models.
  — *Doctrine* refers to an idea or a set of ideas that that are accepted or taught.
  — *Feminine* describes qualities or characteristics that are generally attributed to a woman; *masculine* describes qualities or characteristics that are generally attributed to a man.

Review:
-ine is unaccented when it says /ĭn/.
-ine is accented when it says /ēn/.

DIFFERENTIATING INSTRUCTION If students need additional practice determining accented syllables, do a listening activity. Have students create two cards, one with the number 1 on it and one with the number 2 on it. Then read a selection of List 19 words syllable by syllable. Have students repeat each word. Then have them raise the number 1 card if the primary accent is on the first syllable and the number 2 card if the primary accent is on the second syllable.

Spelling

OBJECTIVE *Students will isolate, pronounce, and spell syllables that are parts of list words.*

Practice Page **19E**

- Have students complete 19E, making sure they understand the directions for each activity. For Activity 1, dictate the following words. Make sure students say each word, isolate the missing syllable(s), and say the whole word as they write it.
  DICTATION: 1. active; 2. captive; 3. relative; 4. positive; 5. office; 6. cowardice; 7. furnace; 8. famine; 9. feminine; 10. determine; 11. medicine; 12. bargain; 13. sardine; 14. gasoline

STEP 3 Work with the Whole Word

Reading

OBJECTIVE *Students will apply accent patterns to read list words correctly.*

Practice Page **19F**

- Review accent patterns. Point out that most two- and three-syllable words are accented on the first syllable, but that three-syllable words with a prefix, root, and suffix are accented on the second syllable.

- Display the words *native* and *positive,* and have students read each word aloud with you as they listen for the accented syllable in each. Have volunteers write each word syllable by syllable and draw a box around the accented syllable, as shown below.

  [na] tive   [pos] i tive

- Have students complete 19F, making sure they understand the directions. You may wish to suggest to students that they mark the accented syllables in the word bank before writing the words under the headings.

Practice Page 19G

Review:
Sometimes *-ine* is unaccented and says /ĭn/ as in *engine.*
Other times *-ine* says /ēn/ as in *magazine.*

- Display the words *marine* and *medicine,* and underline the *-ine* ending in each. Have volunteers identify what *-ine* says in each word.
- Have students complete 19G, making sure they understand the directions.

DIFFERENTIATING INSTRUCTION If students need reinforcement correctly pronouncing words with the *-ine* ending, provide additional practice. Write each of the List 19 words with this ending on a card. Tell students that you will hold up a card and pronounce the word on it two ways using /ĭn/ and /ēn/. Then, as you pronounce the choices a second time, have students give a "thumbs up" for the correct pronunciation and a "thumbs down" for the incorrect pronunciation. Then display the cards randomly, and have students take turns reading each word aloud.

Spelling

OBJECTIVE *Students will spell list words with special attention to schwa endings.*

Practice Page 19H

Review:
The unaccented endings *-ine* and *-ain* occur in final syllables and have the same sound: /ĭn/.

- Display the following examples. Guide students to add *-ine* or *-ain* to make a real word.

  eng___   capt___

- Remind students that if they don't know the correct spelling right away to try both endings and go with the one that looks right.
- Have students complete 19H, making sure they understand the directions.

Practice Pages 19I–19J

Review:
The unaccented endings *-ice* and *-ace* have the same sound: /ĭs/.

- **EXCEPTION:** Display the word *police* and read it aloud, underlining *-ice* as you say it. Explain that *police* is an exception because the *-ice* ending is accented and says /ēs/.
- Have students complete 19I and 19J, making sure they understand the directions.

STEP 4 Work with Words in Context

Comprehension

OBJECTIVE *Students will pair list words with definitions. They will complete sentences using list words and work with parts of speech.*

Practice Pages 19K–19L

- Have students complete 19K and 19L, making sure they understand the directions for each activity. Have them use a dictionary or work with a partner as necessary.

Practice Pages 19M–19N

Review:
A *noun* is a word that refers to a person, place, thing, or idea.
A *verb* is a word that shows action.
An *adjective* is a word that describes a noun.

- Have students complete 19M and 19N, making sure they understand the directions for each activity. Have students use a dictionary or work with a partner as necessary.
- For Activity 2 on 19N, tell students that they may use another form of the verbs as they write their sentences.

Practice Pages 19O–19P

- Have students complete 19O and 19P, making sure they understand the directions for each activity. For Activity 1 on 19O, you may wish to read the paragraphs aloud with students as they underline the words.

Reading and Spelling Skill Check

OBJECTIVE *Students will read words from List 19 with 90 percent accuracy and record their progress on the Accuracy Checklists. Students will spell ten words from List 19 with 90 percent accuracy and record their progress on the Accuracy Checklists.*

Practice Page 19Q

- Have students complete Activities 1–3, making sure they understand the directions.

DIFFERENTIATING INSTRUCTION For students who need fluency practice, ask them to read the sentences in Activity 1 on 19Q silently after they have circled the words. Then have them improve their fluency by reading the sentences aloud to a partner several times.

- For Activity 2 on 19Q, choose three sentences from the first activity to dictate. Have students write the sentences on a separate piece of paper.
- For Activity 3 on 19Q, challenge students to use ten List 19 words in a brief narrative or descriptive paragraph. Encourage them to be creative.

STEP 5 Monitor Progress to Increase Reading and Spelling Accuracy

Reading and Spelling Skill Check

OBJECTIVE *Students will read words from List 19 with 90 percent accuracy and record their progress on the Accuracy Checklists. Students will spell ten words from List 19 with 90 percent accuracy and record their progress on the Accuracy Checklists.*

- The fourth activity on 19Q is a reading and spelling skill check.
- For each student, make two copies of **List 19/Reading Skill Check, Form A or B** (page 109). (You may also select ten words of your choice.) Give a copy to the student and ask him or her to read the words aloud to you as you indicate errors and omissions on the second copy. Share the student's performance with him or her, and have the student record the performance on the **Accuracy Checklist.**
- Provide students with a copy of the **Spelling Skill Check** (page 112). Select ten words from the list or dictate the words below. Share students' performance with them, and have students record their performance on the **Accuracy Checklist.**
  DICTATION: 1. negative; 2. examine; 3. machine; 4. notice; 5. creative; 6. engine; 7. routine; 8. surface; 9. medicine; 10. office

ASSESSMENT If students do not achieve 90 percent accuracy, or if reading and/or spelling accuracy are not improving, more practice should be done on the learning steps. Error analysis can help pinpoint the areas of concern. Skill checks should be repeated until students have achieved 90 percent accuracy or better.

STEP 6 Monitor Progress to Build Reading Proficiency

Word Proficiency

OBJECTIVE *Students will read list words with speed and accuracy.*

- The fifth activity on 18Q is a word proficiency assessment.
- Once students have demonstrated that they can read a selection of List 19 words untimed with 90 percent accuracy, they should work on increasing reading speed by doing frequent rate timings.
- Use a stopwatch or second hand to time each student as he or she reads the list for a minute. A warm-up timing can be used for practice before doing a second "official" timing. If the student finishes the list in less than a minute, he or she should return to the beginning and continue to read until time is up.
- Have students record performance on the **Word Proficiency Graph,** indicating the number of words read correctly in a minute as well as the number of errors. A goal of 45 to 50 words per minute with two or fewer errors on two of three consecutive days is realistic for most students; however, goals should be individualized as appropriate.

ASSESSMENT If a student makes more than four errors on timed readings, discontinue timing the student and focus your instruction instead on reading accuracy. Identify and analyze errors and concentrate your teaching on the specific problem areas. If errors are minimal but the student is still not meeting projected goals, he or she probably needs more practice with the words. Marked improvement can often be made if the word list is practiced at home.

Passage Comprehension and Fluency

OBJECTIVE *Students will read a passage with accuracy and at a reasonable rate, with attention to expression and phrasing, and then answer vocabulary and comprehension questions about it. Students will do repeated readings of that passage to build fluency.*

Practice Page 19R

A Real Bargain? • 152 words

Passage Comprehension

- Have students look at Activity 1. Tell them they are going to read a passage that includes several List 19 words.
- Direct students to the words at the top of the page. Have students practice List 19 Words and Review Words by reading them aloud. Introduce Passage Words by reading them aloud, and give students time to read them with accuracy. Review meanings of words as necessary.
- Have students read the passage and answer the questions independently.
- For students who need additional help, provide support as necessary by identifying unknown words or pointing out the part of the passage where an answer can be found.

Fluency

- Students will be evaluated for fluency individually.
- Tell students that for Activity 2, they will be doing repeated readings of the passage to build speed and accuracy.
- Discuss fluency achievement and goals, and have students continue repeated readings until those goals are met. Between timings, have students look over the passage, reread it, and practice any words that caused difficulty.
- If students are being timed for Word Count Per Minute (WCPM), use the **Recording Form for Practice Page 19R** (page 110) to indicate any errors and to determine rate (mark number of words read by student in one minute, minus errors). Note expression and phrasing as appropriate.
- Share WCPM performance and have students record it on the **Fluency Graph.** WCPM goals should be individualized as appropriate according to grade-specific guidelines for oral reading fluency. You may wish to refer to WCPM rates of Hasbrouck and Tindal oral reading fluency data (2005).

REVIEW LIST 15–19

abdomen
absent*
accurate
ambulance
arrival*
Atlantic*
attendance*
benefit*
captain
captive
certain*
certificate
chocolate*
comedy
concentrate
definite*
democrat

determine
diet*
different*
diplomat
elastic
entrance*
envelope*
fantastic*
feminine*
final*
fortunate
fountain
frequent*
furnace*
garlic
gasoline*
gigantic*

granite
hospital*
ignorant*
important*
influence*
inhabit
innocent*
insurance*
justice*
limit*
magazine*
manager
market*
masculine*
moderate
natural*
notice*

occupant
octopus
opposite*
oral
panic
permanent*
picnic*
plastic*
pocket
porcupine
positive*
practice*
prejudice*
present*
president*
profit

relative*
removal
residence
reversal
sarcastic
several*
silent*
singular*
terrific*
toilet
vacant*
vaccinate
vaccine
velvet
villain
violent*

Note:

- Words suggested as practical spelling words in Lists 15–17 are indicated with an asterisk (*).

REVIEW LIST 15–19

Review Pages 55–58

- Have students read independently or with you the Review List on page 97.
- Review the endings and syllables covered in Lists 15–19 as necessary. Then have students complete pages 98–100, making sure they understand the directions.
- For Activities 5 and 6, have students work with a partner or use the dictionary.

STEP 5 Monitor Progress to Increase Reading and Spelling Accuracy

Reading and Spelling Skill Check

OBJECTIVE *Students will read and spell words from Review List: 15–19 with 90 percent accuracy and record their progress on the Accuracy Checklists.*

- For each student, make two copies of **Review List: 15–19/Reading Assessment, Form A or B** (page 111). (You may also select ten words of your choice.) Ask the student to read the words aloud as you indicate errors and omissions. Share the student's performance, and have the student record it on the **Accuracy Checklist.**
- Provide students with a copy of the **Spelling Assessment** (page 112). Select ten words from the list or dictate the words below. Share students' performance with them, and have students record their performance on the **Accuracy Checklist.**
  DICTATION: 1. certain; 2. occupy; 3. fantastic; 4. masculine; 5. permanent; 6. benefit; 7. vacant; 8. hospital; 9. relative; 10. furnace

> **ASSESSMENT** Skill checks should be repeated until students have achieved 90 percent accuracy or better.

STEP 6 Monitor Progress to Build Reading Proficiency

Word Proficiency

OBJECTIVE *Students will read list words with speed and accuracy.*

- Once students have demonstrated that they can read a selection of review list words untimed with 90 percent accuracy, they should work on increasing reading speed.
- Use a stopwatch or second hand to time each student as he or she reads the list for a minute. A warm-up timing can be used for practice. If the student finishes the list in less than a minute, he or she should return to the beginning and continue to read.
- Have students record performance on the **Word Proficiency Graph,** indicating the number of words read correctly in a minute as well as the number of errors.

> **ASSESSMENT** If a student makes more than four errors on timed readings, discontinue the timing and focus on reading accuracy. Identify and analyze errors and concentrate your teaching on the specific problem areas.

Teacher Resources

WORD LIST 15 *-al* and *-ic* Endings

-al = /əl/

accidental	funeral	oral
actual	general	original
admiral	global	pedal
animal	hospital	personal
arrival	immortal	petal
capital	internal	plural
cardinal	interval	real
central	legal	removal
coastal	liberal	reversal
coral	local	royal
criminal	loyal	several
decimal	mental	signal
dental	metal	skeptical
dismal	mineral	spinal
eternal	moral	structural
external	mortal	terminal
fatal	national	tidal
federal	natural	trial
final	naval	universal
fiscal	normal	vital
formal	optional	vocal

-ic = /ĭk/

academic	comic	Pacific
acrobatic	critic	panic
allergic	democratic	pathetic
anemic	ecstatic	patriotic
angelic	elastic	phonetic
antic	electric	picnic
apathetic	energetic	plastic
arctic	Eric	prolific
artistic	fantastic	public
athletic	frantic	sarcastic
Atlantic	garlic	skeptic
atomic	geographic	spastic
automatic	gigantic	static
basic	heroic	statistic
catastrophic	ironic	systematic
Cedric	logic	tactic
ceramic	music	terrific
characteristic	mystic	traffic
clinic		

Megawords 3 • List 15 **1**

Practice Page 15A

-al

In single-syllable words, the ending *-al* has a short-*a* sound and says /ăl/. In multisyllabic words, the ending *-al* has a schwa sound and says /əl/.

Example: *final*

A **schwa** /ə/ is a vowel sound similar to the short-*u* sound in *up*. It is found only in unaccented syllables of multisyllabic words.

① **Below are some final syllables of List 15 words. Read them aloud to practice saying /əl/.**

nal	tal	cal
mal	dal	ral
val	sal	bal

-ic

In single-syllable words, the ending *-ic* has a short-*i* sound and says /ĭk/. In multisyllabic words, the ending *-ic* also has a short-*i* sound and says /ĭk/.

Example: *picnic*

② **Below are some final syllables of List 15 words. Read them aloud to practice saying /ĭk/.**

ic	mic	nic
lic	fic	ric
tic	sic	pic

③ **Spell the List 15 ending that says /əl/.** al

④ **Spell the List 15 ending that says /ĭk/.** ic

Practice Page 15B

-al

The unaccented ending *-al* has the schwa sound and says /əl/.

Example: *final*

① **Say the syllables to read the whole word. Then write the word.**

or al	oral	e ter nal	eternal
ti dal	tidal	ex ter nal	external
dis mal	dismal	ar ri val	arrival
na val	naval	per son al	personal
pet al	petal	skep ti cal	skeptical
vi tal	vital	ad mir al	admiral
plur al	plural	gen er al	general

② **Match the syllables to make real words. Then say the words as you write them. Make two words for each group.**

lo / mor / vi — tal	sig / fi / le — nal	plas / lo / fis — cal
mortal	signal	local
vital	final	fiscal
re / for / dis — mal	tri / cho / mor — al	met / roy / glo — al
formal	trial	metal
dismal	moral	royal

Practice Page 15C

-ic

The unaccented ending *-ic* says /ik/. The accent is on the syllable just before the *-ic* ending.
Example: *picnic*

① Draw a box around the accented syllable. Say the syllables to read the whole word. Then write the word.

Syllables	Word	Syllables	Word
[arc] tic	arctic	[mys] tic	mystic
[tac] tic	tactic	[stat] ic	static
[an] tic	antic	[ba] sic	basic
ter [rif] ic	terrific	cer [am] ic	ceramic
gi [gan] tic	gigantic	pro [lif] ic	prolific
sar [cas] tic	sarcastic	he [ro] ic	heroic
an [gel] ic	angelic	ath [let] ic	athletic
ec [stat] ic	ecstatic	i [ron] ic	ironic

② In these words, the first syllable has the schwa sound /ə/, and the second syllable has the accent. Draw a box around the accented syllable. Say the syllables to read the whole word. Then write the word.

Syllables	Word	Syllables	Word
a [tom] ic	atomic	a [ne] mic	anemic
sta [tis] tic	statistic	pa [thet] ic	pathetic
al [ler] gic	allergic		

③ Draw a box around the accented syllable in these four-syllable words. Say the syllables to read the whole word. Then write the word.

Syllables	Word	Syllables	Word
en er [get] ic	energetic	ac ro [bat] ic	acrobatic
pa tri [ot] ic	patriotic	dem o [crat] ic	democratic
ge o [graph] ic	geographic	cat a [stroph] ic	catastrophic
ap a [thet] ic	apathetic	sys tem [at] ic	systematic

Practice Page 15D

① Your teacher will dictate twelve words. Spell the missing syllable(s), and then write the whole word.

1. or al — oral
2. traf fic — traffic
3. mor al — moral
4. tri al — trial
5. fu ner al — funeral
6. e lec tric — electric
7. per son al — personal
8. ter rif ic — terrific
9. hos pit al — hospital
10. ge o graph ic — geographic
11. sys tem at ic — systematic
12. cat a stroph ic — catastrophic

② Fill in the missing ending *-al* or *-ic*. Then write the whole word.

Syllables	Word	Syllables	Word
gi gan t ic	gigantic	e lec tr ic	electric
in ter n al	internal	re ver s al	reversal
au to mat ic	automatic	min er al	mineral
ar tis t ic	artistic	ad mir al	admiral
crim in al	criminal	pa thet ic	pathetic
ec stat ic	ecstatic	car din al	cardinal

③ QUICK CHECK Have another student test you on spelling these words.

My score: ____ /____ words correct

Practice Page 15E

① **Read the clues. Fill in the missing words that have *-al* or *-ic* endings.**

spastic	critic	panic	petal
pedal	arctic	tidal	naval
signal	antic	tactic	oral

Clue	Answer
someone who criticizes	critic
spoken; related to the mouth	oral
related to the navy	naval
part of a flower	petal
sign or gesture	signal
helps your foot propel a bike	pedal
related to the North Pole	arctic
silly and stupid act	antic
sudden fright or terror	panic
related to the tides	tidal
planned strategy	tactic
related to a muscle spasm	spastic

Parts of Speech

Words that end in *-ic* or *-al* can be nouns or adjectives.

Nouns refer to people, places, things, or ideas *(child, bedroom, car, perfection).*

Adjectives are words that describe nouns *(lively, pretty, large, swift).*

② **Write a noun or an adjective from Activity 1 to make a common phrase.**

movie critic — rose petal

bicycle pedal — naval officer

arctic climate — tidal wave

Practice Page 15F

Review

The unaccented ending *-al* says /əl/ as in the word *final.*

Accent Patterns: Words with *-al* Endings

In two-syllable words with *-al* endings, accent the first syllable.

In three-syllable words, accent the first syllable. If that doesn't make a recognizable word, shift the accent to the second syllable.

① **Read each word aloud, and listen for the accented syllable. Then write the words syllable by syllable under the correct headings. Write the accented syllables in the boxes.**

moral	reversal	trial	terminal	animal	criminal
vital	removal	immortal	eternal	arrival	

Accent the First Syllable

[mor]	al	[an]	i	mal
[tri]	al	[crim]	i	nal
[vi]	tal	[ter]	min	al

Accent the Second Syllable

im	[mor]	tal
re	[ver]	sal
e	[ter]	nal
ar	[ri]	val
re	[mo]	val

Practice Page 15G

Review

The unaccented ending *-ic* says /ĭk/ as in *picnic.*

Accent Patterns: Words with *-ic* Endings

In words with *-ic* endings, the accent is always on the syllable ***just before*** the *-ic* ending, no matter how many syllables are in the word.

① **Read each word aloud, and listen for the accented syllable. Then write the words syllable by syllable under the correct headings.**

pathetic	critic	characteristic
mystic	patriotic	energetic
geographic	ironic	gigantic

Accent the First Syllable

[mys] tic

[crit] ic

Accent the Second Syllable

pa [thet] ic

i [ron] ic

gi [gan] tic

Accent the Third Syllable

ge o [graph] ic

pa tri [ot] ic

en er [get] ic

Accent the Fourth Syllable

char ac ter [is] tic

Practice Page 15H

Review

Nouns are words that refer to people, places, things, or ideas *(child, bedroom, car, perfection).*

Adjectives are words that describe nouns *(lively, pretty, large, swift).*

When the *-ic* ending is added to a noun, the word becomes an adjective and the accent pattern changes. The accent moves to the syllable just before the *-ic* ending.

Example: *he´ ro* ⟶ *he ro´ ic*

① **Read the following word pairs. Draw a box around the accented syllable in each adjective, and then write the adjective.**

Noun	Adjective	
artist	ar [tis] tic	artistic
athlete	ath [let] ic	athletic
angel	an [gel] ic	angelic
sarcasm	sar [cas] tic	sarcastic
irony	i [ron] ic	ironic
allergy	al [ler] gic	allergic
ecstasy	ec [stat] ic	ecstatic
acrobat	ac ro [bat] ic	acrobatic
system	sys tem [at] ic	systematic
energy	en er [get] ic	energetic
apathy	ap a [thet] ic	apathetic
patriot	pa tri [ot] ic	patriotic
character	char ac ter [is] tic	characteristic
geography	ge o [graph] ic	geographic
democracy	dem o [crat] ic	democratic

Practice Page 15I

Accent Patterns and Parts of Speech

When the *-al* ending is added to a noun, it may change the word to an adjective. When this happens, the accent pattern may change.

- In two-syllable words with *-al* endings, the accent stays on the first syllable.
- In words with three or more syllables, accent the first syllable. If that doesn't make a recognizable word, keep shifting the accent to the next syllable until it makes a word you recognize.

1 **Read the following word pairs. Draw a box around the accented syllable in each adjective, and then write the adjective.**

Noun	Adjective	
coast	[coast] al	coastal
fate	[fa] tal	fatal
music	[mu] si cal	musical
globe	[glo] bal	global
accident	ac ci [den] tal	accidental
spine	[spi] nal	spinal
critic	[crit] i cal	critical
person	[per] son al	personal
tide	[ti] dal	tidal
comic	[com] i cal	comical
origin	or [ig] i nal	original
structure	[struc] tur al	structural
universe	u ni [ver] sal	universal
skeptic	[skep] ti cal	skeptical
navy	[na] val	naval
option	[op] tion al	optional

Practice Page 15J

1 **Complete each sentence with a word from List 15. The missing words are adjective forms of the nouns in italics. Remember to watch your spelling.**

1. When someone uses *sarcasm,* they are making a sarcastic remark.
2. An *athlete* who works out all the time has an athletic body.
3. A *patriot* who salutes the flag is doing a patriotic act.
4. A teacher who is full of *energy* would be described as energetic.
5. A terrible *catastrophe,* such as a flood, is a catastrophic event.
6. *Acrobats* are graceful and do many acrobatic stunts.
7. If you have a fur *allergy,* you may be allergic to many kinds of pets.
8. Someone who is bored and shows a lot of *apathy* is an apathetic person.
9. A person who practices criminal law works to defend the people who are charged with a *crime*.
10. Something that lasts for *eternity* is eternal.
11. Someone who is good at playing *music* has musical talent.
12. A film *critic* is a person who reviews films and is very critical of them.
13. An *accident* is not done on purpose, so it is accidental.
14. A *comic* tells funny and comical stories.
15. When people live by the *coast,* they live in coastal areas.
16. A *skeptic* asks a lot of questions and is very skeptical of things.

Practice Page 15K

Proofreading Practice

Two of the List 15 words are misspelled in each sentence. Rewrite the whole sentence, and spell the words correctly.

1. The trafic was so dismel that we had no real chance of getting to the airport on time.
   The traffic was so dismal that we had no real chance of getting to the airport on time.
2. The admirul was in charge of a navil submarine that had been all over the Atlantic.
   The admiral was in charge of a naval submarine that had been all over the Atlantic.
3. The miner was ecstatic when he found a jigantic piece of a rare metul.
   The miner was ecstatic when he found a gigantic piece of rare metal.
4. Corul can be found in many costal areas along the Pacific.
   Coral can be found in many coastal areas along the Pacific.
5. The lokal food critic was teriffic at finding us great places to eat.
   The local food critic was terrific at finding us great places to eat.
6. Cedric was being patriatik when he sang the Nashunal Anthem.
   Cedric was being patriotic when he sang the National Anthem.
7. When Eric found out he had to give a publik speech, he became frantick.
   When Eric found out he had to give a public speech, he became frantic.
8. Jon was sceptical that he could win his leagle battle if his case went to trial.
   Jon was skeptical that he could win his legal battle if his case went to trial.

Practice Page 15L

① **Complete the puzzle with words from the box.**

electric	hospital	gigantic	music	fantastic
automatic	funeral	personal	traffic	capital
natural	actual	petal	democratic	

Across
1. type of government in the U.S.
5. opposite of fake
8. charged with electricity
10. a place for sick people
11. having to do with nature
12. part of a flower
13. cars moving on a road

Down
2. what you hear on the radio
3. a ceremony to bury the dead
4. huge
5. works by itself
6. private
7. great, wonderful
9. city that holds a state's government

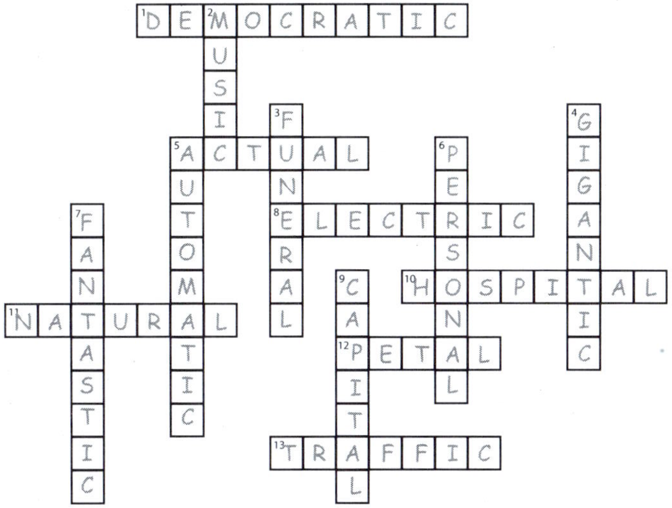

Practice Page 15M

① **Draw an arrow from the underlined adjective to the noun it describes.**

1. Steven is a prolific writer with more than twenty novels to his credit.
2. The fans were ecstatic when their team won the game.
3. Earthquakes, floods, and tornadoes are all catastrophic events.
4. The quiz was optional, but many students took it anyway.
5. The expression on the wounded puppy's face was pathetic.
6. The patriotic soldier was willing to die for his country.
7. Cedric's mental error caused him to get an easy question wrong.
8. The teacher was discouraged by the number of apathetic students in his classroom.
9. Erica was skeptical of Jason's get-rich-quick lottery scheme.
10. Eric's sarcastic comment to his sister about her new haircut upset her.

② **Read the definitions. Choose the correct word from Activity 1, and write it on the line.**

can be chosen but is not required	optional
having a doubting attitude	skeptical
loving one's country	patriotic
pitiful, evoking sympathy	pathetic
producing a lot of something	prolific
extremely happy or excited	ecstatic
disastrous, terrible	catastrophic
cutting or critical in tone	sarcastic
having to do with the mind	mental
showing no interest or emotion; indifferent	apathetic

Practice Page 15N

① **Read the definitions. Choose the correct word from the box, and write it on the line.**

external	mortal	vital	immortal
fatal	written	internal	oral

having to do with the outside	external
having to do with the inside	internal
spoken or related to the mouth	oral
put in words on paper	written
subject to death	mortal
exempt from death	immortal
deadly	fatal
related to life	vital

② **Fill in the blanks with the words from Activity 1.**

1. In Greek mythology, Zeus, Athena, and Poseidon were considered to be immortal.
2. Many students get nervous about giving oral presentations in front of a large number of people.
3. The nurse checked my vital signs, including my pulse and blood pressure.
4. Kate cannot remember anything unless it is written down.
5. Though we are mortal, we don't think about death.
6. Internal medicine deals with the nonsurgical treatment of diseases in the body.
7. The fatal accident left three people dead.
8. Some students need external motivators, such as money or other rewards, to get good grades.

Practice Page 15o

① Read the sentences and circle all the List 15 words.

1. The Atlantic and the Pacific are gigantic oceans.
2. Eric was a loyal and energetic naval officer.
3. There would be less traffic if people would take public transportation instead of their personal cars.
4. The final trip ended with a frantic arrival at the hospital.
5. Several of the critics thought that the music was awful.
6. The coral reefs along the coastal shelf are fantastic.
7. The admiral had dental surgery at the naval clinic.
8. Cedric thinks that he is allergic to garlic.
9. Everyone started to panic when the criminal held up the bank teller.
10. An electric storm caused the central part of the state's capital to lose power.
11. The angelic sound of the vocalist is characteristic of her style.
12. The prolific author wrote terrific novels about heroic and patriotic acts.
13. The school board was skeptical that voters would fund academic needs over athletic interests.

② Your teacher will dictate three of the sentences above. Write them on a blank piece of paper.

③ Write a short story or descriptive paragraph using ten words from List 15. Be creative!

Reading & Spelling Skill Check

Demonstrate your accuracy in reading and spelling List 15 words. Your teacher will select ten words to read and ten words to spell. Record your scores on the Accuracy Checklist. Work toward 90–100 percent accuracy.

Word Proficiency

Now build up your reading proficiency with List 15 words. Decide on your rate goal with your teacher. Record your progress on the Word Proficiency Graph.

My goal for reading List 15 is ____ words per minute with two or fewer errors.

Practice Page 15p

① Practice the words, read the passage, and then answer the questions.

List 15 Words			Review Words	Passage Words	
naval	Atlantic	dismal	hero	African	Louis
Royal	loyal	central	members	American(s)	businessman
coastal	patriotic			parents	figure

James Forten

James Forten was an African American hero. He was born to free parents in 1766—a time when few black Americans were free. When James was ten, Americans went to war to be free of British rule.

At the age of fourteen, James went to serve on a naval ship, the Royal Louis. The ship sailed along the coastal shores and cruised the Atlantic. James worked as a powder boy. His job was to bring gun powder to the ship's large guns.

One day a British ship took over James's ship. Most of the time, when the British took over a ship, they sold black crew members as slaves. But James made friends on the British ship. The British told him they would free him if he swore to be loyal to their side. James was too patriotic and said no. So the British kept him for seven dismal months.

James was let go after the war. He became a wealthy businessman, and he used his wealth to help fellow blacks. While not a central figure in the war, James is a central figure in African American history.

1. Which two words from the text both mean "true to a cause or person"? loyal
2. Why might James have been scared when his ship was taken over by the British? He might have been worried that he would be sold as a slave.
3. What did James do after the war? He became a wealthy businessman, and he used his wealth to help fellow blacks.

② **FLUENCY** Record your progress on the Fluency Graph on page 106.

My goal for reading the passage is ____ words per minute with two or fewer errors.

WORD LIST 16 *-it, -ite, -et,* and *-ate* Endings

-it = /ĭt/ or /ət/*

audit
benefit
biscuit
credit
debit
deposit
explicit
habit
implicit
inhabit
inherit
inhibit
limit
orbit
profit
prohibit
unit

-et = /ĭt/ or /ət/*

banquet
basket
Bridget
bucket
budget
closet
cricket
diet
fidget
gadget
jacket
market
planet
pocket
poet
prophet
quiet
racket
rocket
target
toilet
trumpet
velvet
violet
wallet

-ite = /ĭt/ or /ət/*

composite
definite
exquisite
favorite
granite
hypocrite
indefinite
opposite
prerequisite
requisite
respite

-ate = /ĭt/ or /āt/**

advocate
appropriate
approximate
delegate
deliberate
elaborate
estimate
graduate
moderate
separate

-ate = /ĭt/ or /ət/*

accurate
affectionate
agate
certificate
chocolate
climate
confederate
delicate
desperate
fortunate
illiterate
immaculate
immediate
literate
obstinate
pirate
private
senate

-ate = /āt/

abdicate
accelerate
accumulate
candidate
compensate
concentrate
congratulate
donate
escalate
evaporate
illustrate
isolate
liberate
ornate
precipitate
stimulate
tolerate
vaccinate
validate
violate

* These words can be pronounced both ways, /ĭt/ or /ət/. This lesson uses /ĭt/, but either pronunciation is correct.
** These words can be pronounced both ways, /ĭt/ or /āt/, depending upon whether they are used as verbs, adjectives, or nouns.

Practice Page 16A

-it, -et, -ite, and -ate

In single-syllable words, the endings *-it* and *-et* have short-vowel sounds, and the endings *-ite* and *-ate* have long-vowel sounds.

In multisyllabic words, the endings *-it, -et, -ite,* and *-ate* usually have the *same* vowel sound, short *i*. These endings usually say /ĭt/.

Examples: *qui<u>et</u>, oppos<u>ite</u>*

In multisyllabic words, the ending *-ate* can also say /āt/.

Example: *don<u>ate</u>*

(1) **Below are some final syllables of List 16 words. Read them aloud to practice saying /ĭt/.**

-it	-et	-ite	-ate
fit	get	site	late
dit	ket	crite	date
bit	vet	nite	rate

(2) **Below are some final syllables of List 16 words. Read them aloud to practice saying /āt/.**

mate gate rate cate

(3) **Spell these List 16 endings.**

the endings that can say /ĭt/ at the end of multisyllabic words

-it ______ -et ______ -ite ______ -ate ______

the ending that can say /āt/ at the end of multisyllabic words -ate ______

Practice Page 16B

① Circle the word ending *-it*, *-et*, *-ite*, or *-ate* in each word. Then write the ending on the line.

favorite	ite	pirate	ate
accurate	ate	definite	ite
deposit	it	opposite	ite
planet	et	diet	et
literate	ate	requisite	ite
wallet	et	inherit	it
target	et	agate	ate
cricket	et		

② Say each syllable to read the whole word. Each ending says /ĭt/.

deb it	bas ket
po et	gran ite
pri vate	sen ate
in hab it	def in ite
ac cur ate	des per ate
com pos ite	pro hib it
con fed er ate	cer tif i cate

③ Practice the different sounds of *-ate* in these words. Say each syllable to read the whole word.

***-ate* = /ĭt/**	***-ate* = /āt/**
sep a rate	sep a rate
mod er ate	mod er ate
es tim ate	es tim ate
ap prox i mate	ap prox i mate

Practice Page 16C

Review

In two- and three-syllable words, accent the first syllable and pronounce it according to its syllable type. If that doesn't make a recognizable word, accent the second syllable, and pronounce the second vowel according to its syllable type.

① Draw a box around the accented syllable. Say the syllables to read the whole word, and then write the word.

Accent the First Syllable

qui et	quiet	deb it	debit
pri vate	private	pi rate	pirate
prof it	profit	proph et	prophet
au dit	audit	gran ite	granite
op po site	opposite	choc o late	chocolate
ac cur ate	accurate	des per ate	desperate
def in ite	definite	es tim ate	estimate
ob stin ate	obstinate	fa vor ite	favorite
hyp o crite	hypocrite	ben e fit	benefit
sep a rate	separate	del i cate	delicate
for tu nate	fortunate	req ui site	requisite

Accent the Second Syllable

de pos it	deposit	in her it	inherit
in hab it	inhabit	in hib it	inhibit
ex quis ite	exquisite	com pos ite	composite
im pli cit	implicit	ex pli cit	explicit

Practice Page 16D

In four-syllable words, the accent is usually on the second syllable.
Example: *ap pro′ pri ate*

① **Draw a box around the accented syllable. Say the syllables to read the whole word, and then write the word.**

con [fed] er ate	confederate
e [lab] or ate	elaborate
af [fec] tion ate	affectionate
im [me] di ate	immediate
cer [tif] i cate	certificate
im [mac] u late	immaculate
ap [prox] i mate	approximate
de [lib] er ate	deliberate

② **Read the following three- and four-syllable word pairs. Draw a box around the accented syllable in each word.**

[for] tu nate	→	un [for] tu nate
[def] in ite	→	in [def] in ite
[lit] er ate	→	il [lit] er ate
[req] ui site	→	pre [req] ui site

Practice Page 16E

In three- and four-syllable words where *-ate* is pronounced /āt/, the **primary**, or strongest, **accent** is always on the first or second syllable.

In these words, the final syllable (the *-ate* ending) is also accented. This is called the **secondary accent.** It is not as strong as the primary accent, but it is stronger than no accent at all.

Example: *pre cip′ i tate′*

① **Draw a box around the primary accented syllable and underline the secondary accented syllable. Then pronounce and combine the syllables, and write the whole word.**

con [grat] u late	congratulate
[i] so late	isolate
[con] cen trate	concentrate
ac [cu] mu late	accumulate
[ab] di cate	abdicate
[vi] o late	violate
e [vap] or ate	evaporate
[lib] er ate	liberate
[vac] cin ate	vaccinate
in [val] i date	invalidate

Review

In three- and four-syllable words where *-ate* is pronounced /āt/, the **primary accent** is on the first or second syllable and the **secondary accent** is on the final syllable.

Practice Page 16F

The spelling patterns *-ite* and *-ate* commonly spell /ĭt/ at the end of three- and four-syllable words.

① **Add the ending *-ite* or *-ate* to make a real word. Then write the whole word.**

Add *-ite*		**Add *-ate***	
ex qui s_ite_	exquisite	e lab o r_ate_	elaborate
def i n_ite_	definite	im me di _ate_	immediate
fa vor _ite_	favorite	for tu n_ate_	fortunate
hyp o cr_ite_	hypocrite	ac cur _ate_	accurate
req ui s_ite_	requisite	sep a r_ate_	separate

② **Read the definitions. Choose the correct word from Activity 1, and write it on the line.**

two-faced person	hypocrite
most preferred	favorite
sure thing	definite
right away	immediate
correct	accurate
opposite of together	separate
something that is necessary	requisite
beautifully made, lovely	exquisite
carefully planned with many details	elaborate
lucky	fortunate

③ **QUICK CHECK Have another student test you on spelling these words.**

My score: ______/______ words correct

Practice Page 16G

① **Your teacher will dictate fifteen words. Spell the missing syllable(s). Then say the whole word as you write it.**

1.	_pi_ rate	pirate
2.	_pri_ vate	private
3.	_po_ et	poet
4.	pro _hib_ it	prohibit
5.	fa _vor_ ite	favorite
6.	choc _o_ late	chocolate
7.	cer _ti_ fi _cate_	certificate
8.	_def_ in ite	definite
9.	_il_ lus _trate_	illustrate
10.	_es_ ca _late_	escalate
11.	op _po_ site	opposite
12.	in _hab_ it	inhabit
13.	in _her_ it	inherit
14.	_del_ i cate	delicate
15.	ac _cu_ _mu_ late	accumulate

Two of the words in List 16 are homonyms: **profit** and **prophet**. They are pronounced the same but have different spellings and meanings. Learn these homonyms:

profit: money made after expenses are paid

prophet: one who fortells the future

② **Fill in the blanks.**

profit The _prophet_ told the businessman how he

prophet could make a _profit_ on the Internet.

Practice Page 16H

1. Read each word aloud, and listen for the accented syllable. Then write the words syllable by syllable under the correct headings.

poet	concentrate	immaculate	deposit	respite
prohibit	accelerate	hypocrite	candidate	isolate
donate	precipitate	deliberate	banquet	appropriate

Accent the First Syllable

po	et	con	cen	trate
do	nate	hyp	o	crite
ban	quet	can	di	date
res	pite	i	so	late

Accent the Second Syllable

pro	hib	it	
de	pos	it	
ac	cel	er	ate
pre	cip	i	tate
im	mac	u	late
de	lib	er	ate
ap	pro	pri	ate

Practice Page 16I

1. Write the words syllable by syllable under the correct headings.

~~favorite~~	climate	limit	opposite
deliberate	quiet	prerequisite	market
fortunate	benefit	inhabit	indefinite
delicate	jacket	planet	habit
granite	inherit	certificate	closet

-it

1	2	3
hab	it	
lim	it	
ben	e	fit
in	her	it
in	hab	it

-ite

1	2	3	4
gran	ite		
fa	vor	ite	
op	po	site	
pre	re	qui	site
in	def	in	ite

-et

1	2
qui	et
jack	et
plan	et
mar	ket
clos	et

-ate

1	2	3	4
cli	mate		
del	i	cate	
for	tun	ate	
de	lib	er	ate
cer	tif	i	cate

Review

In two- and three-syllable words, the accent is usually on the *(first, second)* syllable.

In four-syllable words, the accent is usually on the *(first, second, third, fourth)* syllable.

Practice Page 16J

When the ending *-ate* says /ĭt/, it is unaccented. The accent is on another syllable.
Example: *cli′ mate, for′ tu nate*

When *-ate* says /āt/, it has a slight secondary accent. Another syllable has the stronger primary accent.
Example: *vi′ o late′*

① **Read the words. Then write them under the correct headings.**

fortunate	stimulate	accurate	confederate
certificate	validate	desperate	accumulate
literate	accelerate	vaccinate	concentrate
immediate	isolate	obstinate	evaporate
precipitate	chocolate	tolerate	affectionate

***-ate* = /ĭt/**	***-ate* = /āt/**
fortunate	precipitate
certificate	stimulate
literate	validate
immediate	accelerate
chocolate	isolate
accurate	vaccinate
desperate	tolerate
obstinate	accumulate
confederate	concentrate
affectionate	evaporate

Practice Page 16K

① **Circle the /ĭt/ ending in each word. Then write the words under the correct headings.**

clim(ate)	qui(et)	blank(et)	favor(ite)
lim(it)	priv(ate)	benef(it)	biscu(it)
defin(ite)	plan(et)	separ(ate)	estim(ate)
mark(et)	depos(it)	jack(et)	targ(et)
fortun(ate)	wall(et)	sen(ate)	cred(it)
oppos(ite)	immedi(ate)	hab(it)	moder(ate)

-it
limit
deposit
benefit
habit
biscuit
credit

-et
market
quiet
planet
wallet
blanket
jacket
target

-ite
definite
opposite
favorite

-ate
climate
fortunate
private
immediate
separate
senate
estimate
moderate

② **QUICK CHECK** Have another student test you on spelling these words.

My score: ______ /______ words correct

Practice Page 16L

① **Read the definitions. Choose the correct word from the box, and write it on the line.**

desperate	definite	delicate	biscuit
immediate	prohibit	certificate	cricket
benefit	obstinate	fortunate	

a type of bread or muffin	biscuit
something that helps; a useful aid	benefit
a small leaping insect that chirps	cricket
dainty, sensitive, breakable	delicate
stubborn	obstinate
beyond hope; causing despair	desperate
certain; clear in meaning	definite
right away	immediate
to forbid	prohibit
written statement that may be used as proof	certificate
having good luck; lucky	fortunate
to move nervously or restlessly	fidget

② **Divide the words below into syllables as shown. Draw a box around the accented syllable and read each word aloud.**

des|per|ate	im|**me**|di|ate	**ben**|e|fit	**def**|i|nite
pro|**hib**|it	**ob**|sti|nate	**del**|i|cate	cer|**tif**|i|cate
fid|get	**bis**|cuit	**crick**|et	**for**|tu|nate

Practice Page 16M

① **Read the definitions. Choose the correct word from the box, and write it on the line.**

deposit	poet	quiet	profit
fidget	market	inherit	diet
violet	orbit		

an eating plan	diet
a person who writes poems	poet
opposite of loud	quiet
a store that sells food	market
bluish-purple color; also a flower	violet
to move nervously or restlessly	fidget
the path of one object in space around another	orbit
money made after expenses	profit
to put money in a bank	deposit
to receive money from a will	inherit

② **Complete the following sentences with some of the words from Activity 1.**

1. Bridget wrote a great poem about going on a ___diet___ and losing weight. She is quite the ___poet___!
2. Be ___quiet___ and still; please do not ___fidget___ so much during the movie.
3. I went to the local ___market___ and bought some ___violet___ napkins for my party.
4. If you ___inherit___ money from a relative, be sure to ___deposit___ it in your savings account.

Practice Page 16N

The ending *-ate* can be pronounced two different ways, depending on whether the word is a noun, a verb, or an adjective.

- When used as a noun or an adjective, the ending says /ĭt/.
- When used as a verb, the ending will say /āt/.

① Fill in the blanks by using each word twice in the same sentence. Then read the sentences aloud, using both pronunciations of the word.

deliberate	advocate	approximate	moderate	appropriate

1. As an __advocate__ for animal rights, Ken would __advocate__ by helping to find homes for stray cats and dogs.
2. How long will the jury __deliberate__? The defendant made a __deliberate__ attempt to appeal to their sympathy.
3. The student council asked the principal to __appropriate__ funds for their cause, but the principal did not think it was __appropriate__.
4. I tried to __approximate__ how much money I would spend for the year, and I came up with an __approximate__ amount.
5. Sharon had __moderate__ success when she __moderate__d the debate.

Proofreading Practice

Two of the List 16 words are misspelled in each sentence. Cross out each misspelled word, and write the correct spelling above it.

1. The ~~crickits~~ crickets in our yard raise such a ~~rackett~~ racket that it is hard to go to sleep at night.
2. Garrett took his ~~wallett~~ wallet out of his ~~jackut~~ jacket pocket and paid cash for the new bed.
3. That gem is so ornate and ~~exquisate~~ exquisite; you should put it in your safe ~~deposet~~ deposit box.

Practice Page 16O

Review

Adjectives are words that describe nouns (people, places, or things).

① Draw an arrow from the underlined adjective to the noun it describes.

1. The eleven Confederate states formed an alliance in 1860.
2. The obstinate child refused to eat her vegetables.
3. A person who can read a newspaper written at a fourth-grade level is literate.
4. In Arkansas, the winters tend to be moderate.
5. The housekeeper made us take off our shoes, so the house was immaculate.
6. The teacher gave explicit directions so we knew exactly what was expected.
7. My boyfriend and I had an implicit agreement not to date other people.
8. We analyzed the composite scores on all four subtests to get the final results.
9. The exquisite necklace had diamonds and pearls set in an original design.
10. The senior class made elaborate plans for the graduation party to include food, entertainment, and a charity drive.

② Read the definitions. Choose the correct word from Activity 1, and write it on the line.

extremely clean; pure	immaculate
beautifully made	exquisite
stubborn	obstinate
clearly presented or expressed	explicit
implied; understood though not stated	implicit
complex; having many details	elaborate
joined by an agreement or treaty	confederate
not extreme; in the middle or average	moderate
able to read	literate
made up of distinct parts	composite

Practice Page 16P

Verbs

Verbs are words that show action.

① **Circle the subject that is performing the action of the underlined verb.**

1. The (king) abdicated his throne when it became clear that his rival had more power.
2. Gasoline (prices) tend to escalate when there is a shortage of oil from the Middle East.
3. Our (ancestors) used to inhabit caves in prehistoric times.
4. (Brian) accumulates so much paper in his notebook that he can never find anything.
5. The (teacher) stimulated our interest in the Vietnam War by inviting war veterans to speak about their experiences.
6. The (students) were inhibited when the principal observed the classroom; they hesitated to say or do anything.
7. (Abraham Lincoln) helped to liberate slaves during the Civil War.
8. (You) must validate your positions or no one will take your arguments seriously.
9. (Bridget) advocates the use of products that are not tested on animals.
10. The (vet) will vaccinate my dog against rabies and Lyme disease.

② **Read the definitions. Choose the correct word from Activity 1, and write it on the line.**

prove something as true	validate
made active; excited	stimulated
formally gave up a position of power	abdicated
increase in number, volume, or extent	escalate
heaps or piles up	accumulates
live in	inhabit
held back or restrained in some way	inhibited
free from bondage or restraint	liberate
inject an antibody to prevent a disease	vaccinate
speaks or acts in favor of something	advocates

Practice Page 16Q

The following adjectives become nouns by dropping the *-ate* and adding *-acy* as an ending.

Adjective Form	Noun Form
Confederate	Confederacy
literate	literacy
illiterate	illiteracy
private	privacy
accurate	accuracy
delicate	delicacy

① **Fill in the blanks with words from the lists above. You will use both the adjective and the noun form of the word in each numbered item.**

1. Please shut my door when you leave. I like to have ___privacy___ when I'm working. I am a very ___private___ person.
2. Even though the ___Confederacy___ lost the Civil War, many southern states still fly the ___Confederate___ flag.
3. The ___literacy___ rate is much lower in Africa than in the United States, where most adults can read. For example, more people in Sudan are ___illiterate___ than are ___literate___. This means that ___illiteracy___ is very high in Sudan.
4. ___Accuracy___ is extremely important if someone is auditing your taxes. If you are not ___accurate___, you could get in trouble with the government.
5. This meal is elegant, and I would love to eat this fine ___delicacy___, but I have a ___delicate___ stomach. I'm worried that it will make me sick.

Practice Page 16R

① For each exercise, choose one adjective, noun, verb, and phrase from the list below. Use all four in a complete and meaningful sentence and write it in the space provided. Use each word or phrase only once.

Adjective	Noun	Verb	Phrase
illiterate	hermit	prohibited	a shack in the woods
fortunate	housekeeper	was donated	cats and dogs in the house
exquisite	agreement	accumulated	by my lawyer
immaculate	student	inhabited	for more reading instructions
explicit	gem	was validated	to the museum
isolated	pirate	advocated	a lot of gold

1. *The isolated hermit inhabited a shack in the woods.*
2. The immaculate housekeeper prohibited cats and dogs in the house.
3. The explicit agreement was validated by my lawyer.
4. The illiterate student advocated for more reading instructions.
5. The exquisite gem was donated to the museum.
6. The fortunate pirate accumulated a lot of gold.

Practice Page 16S

① Read the sentences and circle all the List 16 words.

1. In the closet you will find my wallet in the pocket of the velvet jacket.
2. Please deposit this check separately and credit it to my account.
3. Janet wanted to move to a moderate climate because her health was delicate.
4. The senate held a private meeting to discuss the auditor's report.
5. With a rocket so accurate, we may soon be able to inhabit other planets.
6. Be quiet and do not fidget so I can concentrate on reading this elaborate report.
7. The fortunate delegate accumulated profits from his favorite investment.
8. The approximate value of the exquisite painting was estimated to be $10,000.
9. The illiterate pirate made a desperate attempt to accelerate his reading progress.
10. You will get immediate results if you eliminate chocolate from your diet.
11. My favorite aunt compensates for her long hours by taking a respite on weekends.
12. Bridget advocated for deliberate action during the private court hearing.
13. Congratulate the candidate who has stimulated so much interest in providing appropriate health benefits for the elderly.

② Your teacher will dictate three of the sentences above. Write them on a blank piece of paper.

③ Write a short story or descriptive paragraph using ten words from List 16. Be creative!

Reading & Spelling Skill Check

Demonstrate your accuracy in reading and spelling List 16 words. Your teacher will select ten words to read and ten words to spell. Record your scores on the Accuracy Checklist. Work toward 90–100 percent accuracy.

Word Proficiency

Now build up your reading proficiency with List 16 words. Decide on your rate goal with your teacher. Record your progress on the Word Proficiency Graph.

My goal for reading List 16 is ______ words per minute with two or fewer errors.

Practice Page 16T

① Practice the words, read the passage, and then answer the questions.

List 16 Words		Review Words		Passage Words	
rockets	immaculate	program	person	American	satellite
candidates	orbit	until	later	woman	around
definite	fortunate	people	doctor	image	mission
prohibited	planet	started	studied	photos	Jemison
toilets	climate	ideas		Sullivan	African

Space Firsts for American Women

Sally Ride was the first American woman in space. She was part of the space shuttle program. Until 1981, rockets took people into space. In 1978, candidates started training for shuttle flight. Ride's first flight was in 1983.

Ride had definite ideas about her image. She prohibited photos of her fixing food or cleaning toilets. Every person on a shuttle crew did those tasks, but she felt the world should see her doing more than making the shuttle immaculate.

A year later, Kathy Sullivan became the first American woman to walk in space. She worked on a satellite that was in orbit around Earth. In 1992, she was fortunate to join the first mission to study our planet's climate from space.

That same year, Mae Jemison became the first African American woman in space. Jemison was a doctor. On her mission, she studied how bones grow in space.

1. Which word from the text means "stopped from doing something"? prohibited
2. When did the American space shuttle program start training candidates? The space shuttle program started training candidates in 1978.
3. What had Mae Jemison been before she flew into space? Jemison had been a doctor.

② **FLUENCY** Record your progress on the Fluency Graph.

My goal for reading the passage is ______ words per minute with two or fewer errors.

WORD LIST 17 Middle-Syllable Schwa

a = /ə/	*e* = /ə/	*o* = /ə/	*u* = /ə/ or /yə/
Agatha	Adeline	abdomen	argument
alphabet	antelope	absolute	calculate
buffalo	benefit	acrobat	incubate
Canada	comedy	advocate	instrument
cinnamon	competent	balcony	insulate
emphasize	complement	chocolate	insulin
escalate	congregate	Christopher	occupy
Isabel	correlate	compromise	pendulum
manager	delegate	custody	porcupine
matador	elephant	customer	regular
Melanie	elevate	democrat	singular
metaphor	enemy	diplomat	stimulate
moccasin	envelope	exodus	
ornament	execute	hypnotize	
permanent	integrate	improvise	
pharmacist	Jeremy	innocent	
pharmacy	Madeline	obsolete	
relative	persecute	octopus	
separate	persevere	pantomime	
tentacle	remedy	suffocate	
	segregate		
	supplement		

Practice Page 17A

Middle-Syllable Schwa

Open syllables end in a vowel and usually have long-vowel sounds.

In three-syllable words, sometimes the open middle syllable is unaccented and the vowel has a schwa sound. There are four ways to spell the schwa sound in these middle syllables:

a as in the syllable *ma,* pronounced /mə/. *(pharmacy)*
e as in the syllable *te,* pronounced /tə/. *(integrate)*
o as in the syllable *co,* pronounced /cə/. *(balcony)*
u as in the syllable *su,* pronounced /sə/. *(insulate)*

1. **Below are some middle syllables of List 17 words. Read these syllables aloud to practice the schwa sound.**

ma	pha	fa
na	ca	ra
ta	la	pa
te	gre	re
ple	ve	se
le	ne	pe
co	ro	so
pro	vo	fo
to	no	lo
su	stru	lu

2. **What four vowels spell the schwa sound in the middle syllables of List 17 words?**

a   e
o   u

Practice Page 17B

In List 17 words, the unaccented schwa sound can be spelled with the vowels *a, e, o,* or *u.* When you spell these words, try another vowel if one does not look right.

1. **Write four ways to spell the following middle syllables that have the schwa sound.**

/trə/	might be spelled	tra	tre	tro	tru
/mə/	might be spelled	ma	me	mo	mu
/nə/	might be spelled	na	ne	no	nu
/plə/	might be spelled	pla	ple	plo	plu
/tə/	might be spelled	ta	te	to	tu
/sə/	might be spelled	sa	se	so	su
/prə/	might be spelled	pra	pre	pro	pru

Review

Any vowel can make the schwa sound.

In List 17, the four vowels that make the schwa sound in the middle syllable are a, e, o, and u.

A syllable with a schwa sound is *(accented, unaccented).*

2. **Your teacher will dictate syllables that have the schwa sound. Write the four ways that these syllables can be spelled.**

1.	ra	re	ro	ru
2.	na	ne	no	nu
3.	ta	te	to	tu
4.	a	e	o	u

Practice Page 17C

① Draw a box around the accented syllable. Write the vowel that makes the schwa sound in the unaccented middle syllable. Then write the whole word.

	Vowel	
[an] te lope	e	antelope
[or] na ment	a	ornament
[ab] do men	o	abdomen
[ab] so lute	o	absolute
[com] ple ment	e	complement
[dip] lo mat	o	diplomat
[per] ma nent	a	permanent
[el] e vate	e	elevate
[ten] ta cle	a	tentacle

The letter *u* says either /ə/ or /yə/ in an unaccented middle syllable. After *g* or *c*, *u* says /yə/.

② Draw a box around the accented syllable. Identify if the unaccented middle syllable has a /ə/ or /yə/ sound. Then write the whole word.

	/ə/ or /yə/?	
[in] stru ment	/ə/	instrument
[por] cu pine	/yə/	porcupine
[cal] cu late	/yə/	calculate
[in] su late	/ə/	insulate
[in] su lin	/ə/	insulin
[sin] gu lar	/yə/	singular
[ar] gu ment	/yə/	argument
[in] cu bate	/yə/	incubate

Practice Page 17D

① Your teacher will dictate ten words. Spell the missing syllables. Then say the whole word as you write it.

1.	or	na	ment	ornament
2.	el	e	vate	elevate
3.	al	pha	bet	alphabet
4.	dip	lo	mat	diplomat
5.	cal	cu	late	calculate
6.	cus	to	mer	customer
7.	ben	e	fit	benefit
8.	rel	a	tive	relative
9.	ab	so	lute	absolute
10.	in	stru	ment	instrument

② Your teacher will dictate sixteen more words. Write the words syllable by syllable.

a as /ə/

1.	man	a	ger
2.	per	ma	nent
3.	mat	a	dor
4.	Can	a	da

e as /ə/

5.	an	te	lope
6.	el	e	phant
7.	com	e	dy
8.	en	ve	lope

o as /ə/

9.	ac	ro	bat
10.	oc	to	pus
11.	ab	so	lute
12.	com	pro	mise

u as /yə/ or /ə/

13.	por	cu	pine
14.	ar	gu	ment
15.	in	su	lin
16.	in	stru	ment

Practice Page 17E

① Write the following words syllable by syllable on the lines. Then mark the long, short, and schwa vowels in each one. You do not need to mark *r*-controlled syllables.

	´	ə	
subjugate	sŭb	jə	gāte
metaphor	mĕt	ə	phor
emphasize	ĕm	phə	sīze
elevate	ĕl	ə	vāte
persecute	per	sə	cūte
acrobat	ăc	rə	băt
hypnotize	hўp	nə	tīze
pendulum	pĕn	də	lŭm
improvise	ĭm	prə	vīse
suffocate	sŭf	fə	cāte
octopus	ŏc	tə	pus
singular	sĭn	gə	lar
execute	ĕx	ə	cūte
pharmacist	phar	mə	cĭst

② Divide the words below into syllables as shown. Draw a box around the accented first syllable, mark the middle vowel with a schwa, and read each word aloud.

[ten] tə cle	[in] cə bate	[in] nə cent	[an] tə lope
[bal] cə ny	[man] ə ger	[in] strə ment	[Can] ə da

Review

The accent in these words is on the (first, second) syllable. The middle syllable is (accented, unaccented) and has a (long, schwa) sound.

Practice Page 17F

① Underline the vowel that has the schwa sound in the middle syllable of each word. Then write the words under the correct headings.

innocent	occupy	elephant	relative
benefit	Canada	absolute	argument
customer	alphabet	calculate	envelope

a as /ə/	e as /ə/	o as /ə/	u as /yə/
Canada	benefit	innocent	occupy
alphabet	elephant	customer	calculate
relative	envelope	absolute	argument

② Fill in the vowel that spells the schwa sound in the middle syllable of each word.

env_e_lope	el_e_phant	cust_o_mer	sep_a_rate
rel_a_tive	reg_u_lar	Can_a_da	occ_u_py
perm_a_nent	ben_e_fit	alph_a_bet	dipl_o_mat
inn_o_cent	arg_u_ment	sing_u_lar	

③ Now circle the fifteen words from Activity 2 in the word search below. The words can be found across or down.

I	N	N	O	C	E	N	T	P	E	R	M	A	N	E	N	T	A	S	C	H
W	A	S	C	A	L	P	H	A	B	E	T	D	I	P	L	O	M	A	T	O
U	N	D	C	N	I	S	S	I	N	G	U	L	A	R	F	O	U	N	D	O
N	L	Y	U	A	I	N	A	R	G	U	M	E	N	T	U	N	A	C	C	E
N	T	E	P	D	D	E	N	V	E	L	O	P	E	B	E	N	E	F	I	T
S	Y	L	Y	A	E	L	E	P	H	A	N	T	S	E	P	A	R	A	T	E
L	A	B	C	U	S	T	O	M	E	R	E	L	A	T	I	V	E	L	E	S

④ Write the leftover letters in the blanks below. Work from left to right.

A SCHWA SOUND IS FOUND ONLY IN UNACCENTED SYLLABLES.

Practice Page 17G

① Fill in the correct vowel for the schwa sound, and then write the whole word.

el_e_vate	elevate	choc_o_late	chocolate
com_e_dy	comedy	acr_o_bat	acrobat
el_e_phant	elephant	abs_o_lute	absolute
sep_a_rate	separate	occ_u_py	occupy
perm_a_nent	permanent	calc_u_late	calculate
pharm_a_cy	pharmacy	arg_u_ment	argument
cust_o_dy	custody	int_e_grate	integrate
cust_o_mer	customer	segr_e_gate	segregate
dem_o_crat	democrat	del_e_gate	delegate
instr_u_ment	instrument	Can_a_da	Canada
sing_u_lar	singular	alph_a_bet	alphabet
reg_u_lar	regular	rel_a_tive	relative
env_e_lope	envelope	compr_o_mise	compromise
ben_e_fit	benefit	inn_o_cent	innocent
en_e_my	enemy	abs_o_lute	absolute

② **QUICK CHECK** Have another student test you on spelling these words.

My score: ____/____ words correct

Practice Page 17H

① Complete the puzzle with words from the box.

octopus	abdomen	moccasin	competent
enemy	argument	cinnamon	permanent
pharmacy	execute	insulin	matador

Across
1. the person who fights the bull in a bullfight
7. lasting, fixed, changeless
9. a substance used to treat people with diabetes
10. to put to death; to carry out
11. a store where drugs are sold

Down
1. a soft leather slipper
2. a disagreement; a fight with words
3. a sea animal with eight legs
4. a brown spice
5. the belly; a part of the body
6. well qualified, capable
8. the opposite of a friend

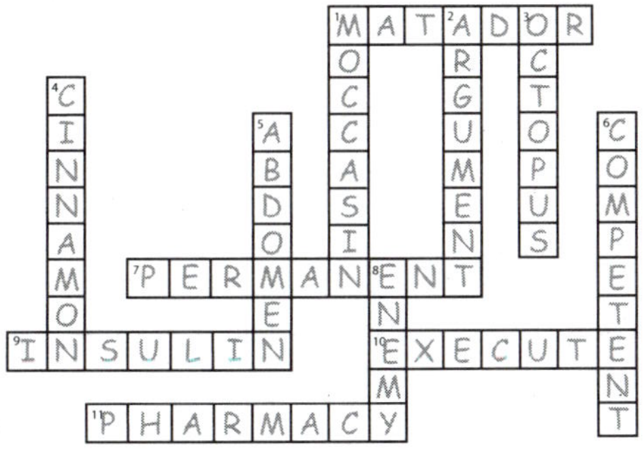

Practice Page 17I

① **Fill in the blanks with the appropriate words below.**

buffalo	obsolete	compromise	Democrats
balcony	acrobat	hypnotize	elephant
calculate	antelope	ornament	innocent
argument	elevate	comedy	suffocate

1. Anthony was ___innocent___; he did not commit the crime.
2. The water ___buffalo___, the ___elephant___, and the ___antelope___ are animals found in Africa.
3. The ___acrobat___ walked on the tightrope in the circus.
4. You can ___calculate___ the age of a tree by counting the rings in the trunk.
5. If you ___elevate___ something, you raise it.
6. Adeline decorated the banquet table with a lovely ___ornament___.
7. The ___Democrats___ and Republicans have conventions to choose their presidential candidates.
8. The two sides talked for hours and got into a heated ___argument___. In the end, they failed to reach a ___compromise___.
9. If you can't get oxygen, you will ___suffocate___.
10. If you put someone in a trance, you ___hypnotize___ them.
11. Jeremy wanted seats close to the stage for the ___comedy___ show, but all he could get were seats up in the ___balcony___.
12. This computer used to be the best on the market, but now it has become ___obsolete___.

Practice Page 17J

Proofreading Practice

Two of the List 17 words are misspelled in each sentence. Rewrite the whole sentence, and spell the words correctly.

1. Antalope, water buffalo, and elephants tend to congragate near water holes.
   Antelope, water buffalo, and elephants tend to congregate near water holes.
2. The custamer had no prescription, but he argued with the pharmecist.
   The customer had no prescription, but he argued with the pharmacist.
3. A matador often needs to be a compatent acrabat.
   A matador often needs to be a competent acrobat.
4. The twins compremised and bought one chocalate and one cinnamon doughnut.
   The twins compromised and bought one chocolate and one cinnamon doughnut.
5. I emphesized that it would be disastrous to fight a porkupine or an octopus.
   I emphasized that it would be disastrous to fight a porcupine or an octopus.
6. The leather moccosins Isabel bought in Canada had lovely beaded ornamants on them.
   The leather moccasins Isabel bought in Canada had lovely beaded ornaments on them.
7. The delugate did his best not to escolate the argument taking place in the meeting.
   The delegate did his best not to escalate the argument taking place in the meeting.
8. I have a reletive who uses a watch as a pendyulum to hypnotize people.
   I have a relative who uses a watch as a pendulum to hypnotize people.

Practice Page 17K

Practice Page 17K

Review

Verbs are words that show action.

① **Replace the underlined word or words with the correct verb from the box. Write the word on the line.**

congregate	segregate	correlated	advocates
integrate	elevated	execute	persevere
benefit	improvise	incubated	

1. In the 1960s, Civil Rights activists sought to mix together people of all races within schools, public transportation, and other public facilities. integrate
2. Teachers often isolate disruptive students from the class. segregate
3. Ostrich eggs should be kept under favorable conditions for hatching for at least two weeks. incubated
4. The students would gain an advantage from a quick break. benefit
5. Brittany and her friends gather together in the front lobby. congregate
6. Melanie speaks up for endangered animals such as wolves. advocates
7. Many citizens believe that we should not put to death criminals under any circumstances. execute
8. The data showed a systematic connection between hearing loss and loud noise. correlated
9. The drama coach encouraged us to create on the spur of the moment a different ending to the play. improvise
10. Because of the serious infection, Isabel's white blood cell count was raised above the normal level. elevated
11. If at first you don't succeed, try, try again. persevere

Practice Page 17L

Practice Page 17L

Review

Nouns are words that refer to people, places, things, or ideas.

① **Replace the underlined words with a word from the box. Write the word on the line.**

custody	remedy	metaphors	insulin
matador	abdomen	delegate	pendulum

1. Shakespeare often uses comparisons where one thing is said to be another to create vivid images. metaphors
2. Agatha thought she was having problems with her appendix because of the pain in her body between her chest and her hips. abdomen
3. The grandfather clock did not keep time well; something was wrong with the suspended piece that swings back and forth. pendulum
4. When the bullfighter raised the red cape, the angry bull charged. matador
5. People who have diabetes have an excess of sugar in their blood and need to inject the hormone that helps the body use sugar to control the disease. insulin
6. The father was hoping to get the duty of taking care of his three young children. custody
7. Jeremy went to the national convention as the person who represents others from his local organization. delegate
8. Isabel could not find an effective medicine or treatment for her cold. remedy

Practice Page 17M

Review

Adjectives are words that describe people, places, things, or ideas.

(1) **Draw an arrow from the underlined adjective to the noun it describes.**

1. After doing a good job on the report, Amy was given a permanent position with the firm.
2. Jon made an innocent mistake when he confused one identical twin with the other.
3. The typewriter may be obsolete, but I still prefer it to the computer.
4. The competent mechanic should be able to fix my car in under an hour!
5. Our regular Wednesday meeting was moved to Friday instead.
6. This pearl necklace has a singular beauty that cannot be matched.

(2) **Read the definitions. Choose the correct underlined word from Activity 1, and write it on the line.**

happening on a steady basis	regular
harmless; not offensive	innocent
excellent; outstanding	singular
lasting indefinitely	permanent
skilled; capable	competent
out of date	obsolete

Practice Page 17N

(1) **Read the sentences and circle all the List 17 words.**

1. Isabel and Adeline had an argument about hospital benefits.
2. The Democrats emphasized the need to compromise.
3. The pharmacist did not advocate the medicine as a remedy for her customer.
4. The octopus was not a permanent resident of the zoo.
5. The porcupine does not have many enemies to persecute it.
6. Madeline used a pendulum as an instrument to hypnotize the manager.
7. The elephant, the buffalo, and the antelope are all majestic animals.
8. It should be mandatory for managers to be competent and execute their jobs well.
9. Jeremy and Christopher had relatives in Canada.
10. The matador had to elevate his leg after he bruised it in the bullfight.
11. A diplomat cannot be absolute; he or she must compromise.
12. Brittany was a regular customer at the pharmacy.
13. The acrobat executed a perfect leap off the balcony as part of a comedy act.
14. The motto "separate but equal" segregates people rather than integrates them.
15. Chocolate is an absolute remedy for a bad day and can elevate anyone's mood.

(2) **Your teacher will dictate three of the sentences above. Write them on a blank piece of paper.**

(3) **Write a short story or descriptive paragraph using ten words from List 17. Be creative!**

Reading & Spelling Skill Check

Demonstrate your accuracy in reading and spelling List 17 words. Your teacher will select ten words to read and ten words to spell. Record your scores on the Accuracy Checklist. Work toward 90–100 percent accuracy.

Word Proficiency

Now build up your reading proficiency with List 17 words. Decide on your rate goal with your teacher. Record your progress on the Word Proficiency Graph.

My goal for reading List 17 is ______ words per minute with two or fewer errors.

Practice Page 17o

1. Practice the words, read the passage, and then answer the questions.

List 17 Words			Review Words		Passage Words	
octopus	tentacles	calculate	elastic	study	invertebrate	feature
acrobat	enemy	alphabet	largest	learned	water	family
relative	singular	perseveres	problem	until	hungry	scientists
						solving

A Smart Invertebrate?

The octopus is an invertebrate, which means it has no bones. It moves through the water like an elastic acrobat. Like its relative the squid, it has eight tentacles. It can shoot out a cloud of black ink at a hungry enemy. Some types of octopus can kill humans or even sharks.

But the most singular feature of an octopus may be its brain. The octopus seems to be very smart—for an invertebrate. In fact, the octopus has the largest brain in the boneless family. It can't calculate square roots or learn the alphabet. But scientists have found it can do easy problem solving.

One study showed that the octopus can tell shapes apart. Another study showed it can learn to play with toys. An octopus in a German zoo even learned to twist the top off a food jar. It perseveres up to an hour until the lid is off.

1. Which word from the text means "a member of the family"? relative
2. How does the octopus defend itself against enemies? It shoots out a cloud of black ink at a hungry enemy.
3. What is one smart thing that an octopus has been known to do? They can do easy problem solving, learn to play with toys, or learn to twist the top off a food jar.

2. **FLUENCY Record your progress on the Fluency Graph.**

My goal for reading the passage is ____ words per minute with two or fewer errors.

REVIEW LIST 15–17

abdomen	compromise	legal
absolute	customer	manager
accidental	deliberate	music
affectionate	donate	national
allergic	electric	original
alphabet	emphasize	planet
argument	enemy	plural
athletic	energetic	private
balcony	favorite	public
benefit	habit	regular
biscuit	heroic	remedy
budget	immediate	separate
central	indefinite	trial
climate	instrument	wallet

Review List 15–17

① **Draw a box around the accented syllable. Say the syllables to read the whole word. Then write the word.**

al [ler] gic	allergic	[bud] get	budget
[em] pha size	emphasize	[do] nate	donate
im [me] di ate	immediate	[bis] cuit	biscuit
ac ci [den] tal	accidental	[man] a ger	manager
af [fec] tion ate	affectionate	[na] tion al	national
de [lib] er ate	deliberate	[pub] lic	public

② **Write the words from Activity 1 under the correct headings.**

Words with Two Syllables	Words with Three Syllables	Words with Four Syllables
budget	allergic	accidental
donate	emphasize	affectionate
biscuit	manager	deliberate
public	national	immediate

Proofreading Practice

Two of the Review List words are misspelled in each sentence. Cross out each misspelled word, and write the correct spelling above it.

1. The ~~custumer~~ customer came to repair his favorite appliance, the ~~electrick~~ electric lawn mower.
2. The regular path of the Moon around Earth affects the ~~climite~~ climate of our ~~plannet~~ planet.
3. The ~~publick~~ public trial was full of complex ~~leagal~~ legal issues.

Review List 15–17

Review

Adjectives are words that describe nouns (people, places, or things).

③ **Draw an arrow from the underlined adjective to the noun it describes.**

1. The original house is more than two hundred years old, but over time new sections have been added or updated.
2. Even the most energetic puppies get tired after an hour of playing at the park.
3. When you talk about more than one, you must use the plural form of the word.
4. The collision of the two cars was accidental, but it may have been avoided if both drivers hadn't been talking on their cell phones.
5. The firefighter's heroic efforts saved the people who had been trapped in the burning building.
6. Since the rain ruined our day at the beach, our plans are indefinite.

④ **Read the definitions. Choose the correct underlined word from Activity 3, and write it on the line.**

full of energy	energetic
not clear or fixed	indefinite
existing first or from the beginning	original
refers to more than one	plural
showing great bravery or courage	heroic
happening by chance	accidental

Review List 15–17

⑤ **Fill in the vowel that spells the schwa sound in each word below.**

en_e_my	favor_i_te	cust_o_mer	abd_o_men
nation_a_l	wall_e_t	priv_a_te	indefin_i_te
hab_i_t	instr_u_ment	balc_o_ny	emph_a_size

⑥ **Complete the puzzle with words from the box.**

athletic	separate	enemy	argument
climate	energetic	alphabet	private

Across

3. opposite of friend
5. the set of letters used to write words
7. a disagreement
8. weather conditions in an area

Down

1. opposite of together
2. relating to sports activities
4. full of energy
6. opposite of public

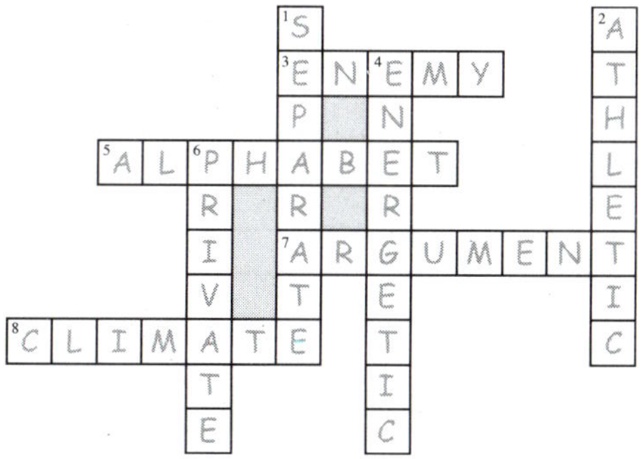

WORD LIST 18 *-ant, -ance, -ent,* and *-ence* Endings

-ant = /ənt/	***-ance*** = /əns/	***-ent*** = /ənt/	***-ence*** = /əns/
abundant	abundance	absent	absence
applicant	acceptance	adjacent	affluence
arrogant	ambulance	affluent	audience
assailant	appearance	agent	competence
assistant	appliance	client	confidence
attendant	arrogance	competent	correspondence
compliant	assistance	confident	dependence
constant	attendance	consistent	difference
defendant	balance	correspondent	essence
defiant	clearance	decent	evidence
distant	compliance	delinquent	excellence
dominant	defiance	dependent	experience
elegant	distance	different	independence
fragrant	dominance	evident	influence
hesitant	elegance	excellent	innocence
ignorant	endurance	frequent	intelligence
important	entrance	independent	magnificence
infant	fragrance	innocent	negligence
inhabitant	hindrance	intelligent	obedience
instant	ignorance	magnificent	preference
malignant	importance	negligent	presence
occupant	instance	obedient	residence
pleasant	insurance	present	reverence
pregnant	perseverance	president	science
resistant	relevance	recent	silence
servant	resistance	resident	violence
significant	significance	reverent	
tolerant	substance	silent	
truant	tolerance	student	
vacant		violent	

-ancy = /əncy/
hesitancy
infancy
malignancy
occupancy
pregnancy
truancy
vacancy

-ency = /əncy/
agency
competency
consistency
decency
delinquency
frequency
presidency
residency

Practice Page 18A

-ant, -ance, -ent, and -ence

In single-syllable words, the endings *-ant, -ance, -ent,* and *-ence* have short-vowel sounds.

In multisyllabic words, the endings *-ant, -ance, -ent,* and *-ence* have the schwa sound. They are always unaccented.

-ant and *-ent* say /ənt/. (*servant, present*)

-ance and *-ence* say /əns/. (*distance, absence*)

1. Below are some final syllables of List 18 words. Read them aloud to practice the /ənt/ and /əns/ endings.

-ant	*-ance*	*-ent*	*-ence*
tant	grance	nent	lence
fant	tance	dent	dence
dant	nance	quent	tence

2. Spell the List 18 endings that say /ənt/ in multisyllabic words.

ant　ent

3. Spell the List 18 endings that say /əns/ in multisyllabic words.

ance　ence

Practice Page 18B

/ənt/ and /əns/

The ending /ənt/ can be spelled either *-ant* or *-ent* as in *servant* and *present*.
The ending /əns/ can be spelled either *-ance* or *-ence* as in *distance* and *absence*.

1. Write two ways to spell the syllables.

/vənt/ might be spelled vant or vent.
/dəns/ might be spelled dance or dence.
/təns/ might be spelled tance or tence.
/ləns/ might be spelled lance or lence.
/dənt/ might be spelled dant or dent.

2. Your teacher will dictate eight syllables with /ənt/ or /əns/. Write two ways each syllable might be spelled.

1. rance or rence
2. dent or dant
3. tance or tence
4. rant or rent
5. lent or lant
6. ant or ent
7. ence or ance
8. lance or lence

3. Fill in the blanks with *-ant* or *-ent*.

***-ant* = /ənt/**	***-ent* = /ənt/**
dis t ant	stu d ent
im por t ant	a g ent
in f ant	fre qu ent
va c ant	ex cel l ent
at ten d ant	pres i d ent
pleas ant	pres ent
sig nif i c ant	in tel li g ent

© EPS • DO NOT DUPLICATE

Practice Page 18C

-ant, -ance, and -ancy

The endings *-ant* and *-ance* contain the schwa sounds /ənt/ and /əns/ as in *distant* and *distance*. The ending *-ancy*, as in *hesitancy*, is a variation of *-ance*.

① **Say each syllable, and then read the whole word. Draw a box around the accented syllable, and mark the vowel long or short.**

Accent the First Syllable

fra grant	fragrant	fra grance	fragrance
ig nor ant	ignorant	ig nor ance	ignorance
dom i nant	dominant	dom i nance	dominance
ar ro gant	arrogant	ar ro gance	arrogance
tol er ant	tolerant	tol er ance	tolerance
tru ant	truant	tru an cy	truancy
va cant	vacant	va can cy	vacancy
hes i tant	hesitant	hes i tan cy	hesitancy
oc cu pant	occupant	oc cu pan cy	occupancy

Accent the Second Syllable

com pli ant	compliant	com pli ance	compliance
at ten dant	attendant	at ten dance	attendance
de fi ant	defiant	de fi ance	defiance
re sis tant	resistant	re sis tance	resistance
sig nif i cant	significant	sig nif i cance	significance
ma lig nant	malignant	ma lig nan cy	malignancy

Practice Page 18D

-ent, -ence, and -ency

The endings *-ent* and *-ence* contain the schwa sounds /ənt/ and /əns/ as in *silent* and *silence*. The ending *-ency*, as in *frequency*, is a variation of *-ence*.

① **Say each syllable, and then read the whole word. Draw a box around the accented syllable, and mark the vowel long or short.**

Accent the First Syllable

pres ent	present	pres ence	presence
vi o lent	violent	vi o lence	violence
neg li gent	negligent	neg li gence	negligence
com pe tent	competent	com pe tence	competence
in no cent	innocent	in no cence	innocence
ev i dent	evident	ev i dence	evidence
de cent	decent	de cen cy	decency
fre quent	frequent	fre quen cy	frequency
pres i dent	president	pres i den cy	presidency

Accent the Second or Third Syllable

o be di ent	obedient	o be di ence	obedience
mag nif i cent	magnificent	mag nif i cence	magnificence
in tel li gent	intelligent	in tel li gence	intelligence
in de pen dent	independent	in de pen dence	independence
cor res pon dent	correspondent	cor res pon dence	correspondence
con sis tent	consistent	con sis ten cy	consistency

Practice Page 18E

① Your teacher will dictate ten words. Spell the missing syllables. Then say the whole word as you write it.

1.	ser	vant		servant
2.	dis	tance		distance
3.	ab	sent		absent
4.	si	lence		silence
5.	ig	nor	ance	ignorance
6.	con	stant		constant
7.	dom	i	nant	dominant
8.	im	por	tant	important
9.	a	gent		agent
10.	pref	er	ence	preference

② Your teacher will dictate sixteen more words. Write the words syllable by syllable under the correct headings.

-ant

	im	por	tant
	de	fen	dant
in	hab	i	tant
sig	nif	i	cant

-ent

	dif	fer	ent
	ex	cel	lent
	res	i	dent
in	de	pen	dent

-ance

	sub	stance
in	sur	ance
ig	nor	ance
am	bu	lance

-ence

	si	lence
neg	li	gence
de	pen	dence
ev	i	dence

Practice Page 18F

① Read each word aloud, and listen for the accented syllable. Then write the words syllable by syllable under the correct headings.

significance	instant	arrogant	client
negligence	abundance	confidence	inhabitant
entrance	intelligent	affluent	compliance
adjacent	malignant	truant	

Accent the First Syllable

en	trance	neg	li	gence
in	stant	ar	ro	gant
tru	ant	con	fi	dence
cli	ent	af	flu	ent

Accent the Second Syllable

ad	ja	cent	
a	bun	dance	
ma	lig	nant	
com	pli	ance	
sig	nif	i	cance
in	tel	li	gent
in	hab	i	tant

Practice Page 18G

① **Write the words in the box under the correct headings.**

important	recent	insurance	distance
president	instant	attendance	attendant
confidence	ignorant	different	violence
frequent	appliance	experience	influence

-ant	***-ance***
important	appliance
instant	insurance
ignorant	attendance
attendant	distance

-ent	***-ence***
president	confidence
frequent	experience
recent	violence
different	influence

② **Fill in the blanks with the correct *-ant, -ent, -ance,* or *-ence* ending. In some cases, two endings are correct. Choose one and write it on the line.**

inf ant	stud ent
import ant/ance	vac ant
sil ent/ence	sci ence
appear ance	influ ence
viol ent/ence	attend ant/ance
differ ent/ence	ess ence

Practice Page 18H

Learn these spelling rules:
-ant becomes *-ance* (*distant* ⟷ *distance*)
-ent becomes *-ence* (*silent* ⟷ *silence*)

① **Change the adjectives that end in /ənt/ into nouns that end in /əns/ and vice versa.**

Adjective *-ant*	⟷	**Noun *-ance***	**Adjective *-ent***	⟷	**Noun *-ence***
distant		distance	silent		silence
ignorant		ignorance	absent		absence
important		importance	present		presence
fragrant		fragrance	independent		independence
elegant		elegance	obedient		obedience
significant		significance	violent		violence
tolerant		tolerance	different		difference
defiant		defiance	excellent		excellence
instant		instance	innocent		innocence
abundant		abundance	intelligent		intelligence
attendant		attendance	confident		confidence
dominant		dominance	correspondent		correspondence

② **Unscramble the syllables to make real words.**

dence con fi	confidence
ap ance pear	appearance
pen de dent	dependent

Review

Words ending in *-ant* or *-ent* are (*nouns, adjectives*).

Words ending in *-ance* or *-ence* are (*nouns, adjectives*).

Practice Page 18I

When /ənt/ or /əns/ follows a hard *c* or *g*, the ending begins with the letter *a (vacant, elegance)*.
When /ənt/ or /əns/ follows a soft *c* or *g*, the ending begins with the letter *e (decent, intelligence)*.

① **Write the words in the box under the correct headings.**

vacancy	agent	arrogant	agency
decent	vacant	negligent	recent
innocent	negligence	magnificent	intelligent
adjacent	applicant	innocence	elegance
elegant	significant	intelligence	arrogance

Hard *c* or *g*	Soft *c* or *g*
vacancy	decent
elegant	innocent
vacant	adjacent
applicant	agent
significant	negligence
arrogant	negligent
elegance	magnificent
arrogance	innocence
	intelligence
	agency
	recent
	intelligent

② **QUICK CHECK** **Have another student test you on spelling these words.**

My score: ____/____ words correct

Practice Page 18J

Proofreading Practice

Two of the List 18 words are misspelled in each sentence. Rewrite the whole sentence, and spell the words correctly.

1. Ms. Torrance teaches an excellant sciance course with frequent field trips.
   Ms. Torrance teaches an excellent science course with frequent field trips.
2. The secret service agents guard the presidant at all public appearences.
   The secret service agents guard the president at all public appearances.
3. I have evidence to show that the job applicant is an inteligent and desent person.
   I have evidence to show that the job applicant is an intelligent and decent person.
4. You should be less arrogent and more tolerant of people with differant opinions.
   You should be less arrogant and more tolerant of people with different opinions.
5. Unless the truent's attendence improves, he will be sent to a school for delinquents.
   Unless the truant's attendance improves, he will be sent to a school for delinquents.
6. It is evident that the presidancy will be determined by indeppendent voters.
   It is evident that the presidency will be determined by independent voters.
7. The ajent was hesitent to have his client sign the contract.
   The agent was hesitant to have his client sign the contract.
8. The defendant became defient when the lawyer claimed that he was a vilent person.
   The defendant became defiant when the lawyer claimed that he was a violent person.

Practice Page 18K

If the adjective form of a word ends in *-ant*, the noun form ends in *-ance* or *-ancy*.
If the adjective form of a word ends in *-ent*, the noun form ends in *-ence* or *-ency*.

① Fill in the blanks with the noun or adjective form of the word in italics.

1. Lawrence was *innocent*, but it was hard to prove his ___innocence___.
2. I noticed Jordan's ___hesitancy___; she was *hesitant* about going alone.
3. Paula gained only thirty pounds while she was ___pregnant___ and felt healthy throughout her *pregnancy*.
4. Ashley was *confident* she could make the audience laugh. Their frequent laughter boosted her ___confidence___.
5. If you see a movie with *violence* in it, do you become ___violent___?
6. The medical *resident* just completed her hospital ___residency___.
7. Christopher seems to be a ___decent___ fellow; he had the *decency* to call and tell us he would be late.
8. It is very *important* that you eat fruits and vegetables; I can't overemphasize the ___importance___ of that.
9. Fido went to *obedience* school to learn to be ___obedient___.
10. The rental *agent* had worked in the ___agency___ for ten years.
11. There was not much *difference* between Dennis and Donovan; the twins were hardly ___different___ at all.
12. There is a ___vacancy___ in that building next to the *vacant* lot.
13. The rose is a ___fragrant___ flower; I like its *fragrance*.
14. ___Infancy___ must be a nice time; most *infants* seem happy.
15. The ___president___ holds the *presidency* for a four-year term.

Practice Page 18L

-ant

Most *-ant* words are either adjectives or nouns. Many of the *-ant* nouns mean "a person who…"

① Read the definitions. Choose the correct word from the box, and write it on the line.

assailant	inhabitant	defendant	servant
applicant	truant	occupant	attendant

- a person who serves others ___servant___
- a person who is defended in a trial ___defendant___
- a person who attends to things ___attendant___
- a person who applies for a job ___applicant___
- a person who inhabits a place ___inhabitant___
- a person who occupies a place ___occupant___
- a person who has a truancy problem ___truant___
- a person who attacks, or assails, someone ___assailant___

-ent

Most *-ent* words are also either adjectives or nouns. Many of the *-ent* nouns also mean "a person who..."

② Read the definitions. Choose the correct word from the box, and write it on the line.

student	correspondent	dependent	resident

- a person who resides, or lives, somewhere ___resident___
- a person who depends on others ___dependent___
- a person who writes to, or corresponds with, others ___correspondent___
- a person who studies or goes to school ___student___

Practice Page 18M

-ence and *-ance*

Words that end in *-ence* or *-ance* are always nouns. These words often have a verb in the root.

① **Fill in the blanks with the noun form of the verb in italics.**

1. When you *enter* a room, you go through an ____________.
2. When you *clear* out your inventory, you have a ____________ sale.
3. When you *insure* your car, you buy ____________.
4. When you *resist*, you show ____________.
5. When you *appear*, you make an ____________.
6. When you *accept* something, you show ____________.
7. When you *prefer* something, you have a ____________.
8. When you *confide* in a friend, you tell him something in ____________.
9. When you *assist* someone, you give ____________.
10. When you *attend* an event, you are in ____________.
11. When you *dominate* something, you show your ____________.
12. When you *obey* a command, you show ____________.
13. When you *comply* with another's wishes, you show ____________.
14. When you *defy* an order, you show ____________.
15. When you *ignore* things, you display ____________.
16. When you *tolerate* something, you show ____________.

Practice Page 18N

① **Fill in the missing parts of speech for each word family below.**

Noun	Verb	Adjective
hesitancy	hesitate	hesitant
defiance	defy	defiant
compliance	comply	compliant
reverence	revere	reverent
dominance	dominate	dominant
tolerance	tolerate	tolerant
excellence	excel	excellent
ignorance	ignore	ignorant
significance	signify	significant
negligence	neglect	negligent
violence	violate	violent
obedience	obey	obedient
difference	differ	different

② **Write three sentences. Use at least two words from Activity 1 in each sentence.**

1. Answers will vary.
2. ____________
3. ____________

Practice Page 18o

① Read the definitions. Choose the correct word from the box, and write it on the line.

present	compliant	intelligent	defiant
independent	ignorant	dependent	absent

agreeable	compliant
resistant	defiant
smart	intelligent
uneducated	ignorant
in attendance	present
not in attendance	absent
relying on someone or something	dependent
free from others' control	independent

② Fill in the blanks with the words from Activity 1.

1. The independent group did not answer to anyone but themselves.
2. When his parents questioned his honesty, Jon became defiant.
3. All team members are present and accounted for.
4. Trent did not mean to make an offensive remark; he was just ignorant of the fact that it was offensive.
5. Our picnic is dependent on the weather; if it rains, the picnic will be cancelled.
6. Katrina's intelligent response to the question made her teacher smile.
7. Jim was compliant with the law, so he was not arrested.
8. If they don't get here soon, they will be marked absent.

Practice Page 18p

① Complete the puzzle with words from the box.

absent	abundance	consistent	delinquent
elegant	evidence	excellent	fragrance
frequency	hesitant	infancy	recent

Across
2. proof of something
8. early childhood
9. not present
10. graceful and stylish
11. outstanding
12. opposite of old or out-of-date

Down
1. the rate at which something occurs
3. a young troublemaker
4. unchanged over a long period of time; steady
5. a large amount of something
6. a pleasant smell
7. unsure; slow to act

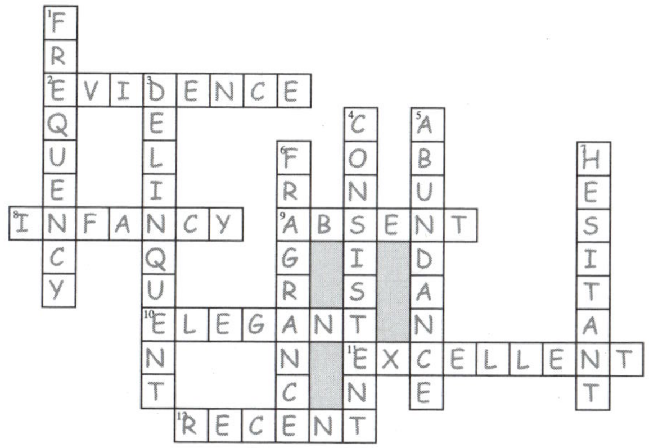

Practice Page 18Q

① **Read the sentences and circle all the List 18 words.**

1. The innocent defendant has no confidence in his lawyer.
2. In this instance, it is important that each student makes an independent decision.
3. The president had evidence that the secret agent was present at the hearing.
4. There is a significant difference between delinquent and decent behavior.
5. The recent violence among the island's inhabitants is a hindrance to the peace effort.
6. The client would prefer term insurance.
7. The parking attendant was defiant in the presence of the arrogant correspondent.
8. The silence in the vacant house was evidence that no one lived there.
9. With her experience, Ms. Clemens should be able to get a decent job.
10. The long distance runner showed endurance and perseverance during the marathon.
11. Delinquency is usually the result of defiant rather than compliant behavior.
12. The job applicant appeared to be both confident and competent during the interview.

② **Your teacher will dictate three of the sentences above. Write them on a blank piece of paper.**

③ **Write a short story or descriptive paragraph using ten words from List 18. Be creative!**

Reading & Spelling Skill Check

Demonstrate your accuracy in reading and spelling List 18 words. Your teacher will select ten words to read and ten words to spell. Record your scores on the Accuracy Checklist. Work toward 90–100 percent accuracy.

Word Proficiency

Now build up your reading proficiency with List 18 words. Decide on your rate goal with your teacher. Record your progress on the Word Proficiency Graph.

My goal for reading List 18 is ______ words per minute with two or fewer errors.

Practice Page 18R

① **Practice the words, read the passage, and then answer the questions.**

List 18 Words		Review Words		Passage Words	
dependent	important	everyone	fuels	energy	barrels
significant	dependence	plastic	prepare	supply	because
abundant	frequency	never		million	hydrogen
constant	appliances				
recent	excellent				

Cutting Dependence on Oil

The U.S. is dependent on oil for most of its energy. Why is this significant? Because what was once an abundant and constant supply will dry up one day.

In recent years, the U.S. has used close to twenty million barrels of oil a day. It is now important for everyone to make smart choices about energy use to cut dependence on oil.

We can cut back on the frequency of our oil use. We can use bikes and not cars. We can turn down home heaters and use appliances that burn less oil. Even stopping the use of plastic bags can help because plastic is made from oil.

We will need to find new forms of energy, too. Sun and wind power are excellent choices because they are abundant and will never run out. New car fuels such as hydrogen may also help. Smart choices now will prepare us for the future.

1. Which word from the text means "plentiful"? abundant
2. In recent years, how many barrels of oil does the U.S. use a day? The U.S. uses close to twenty million barrels of oil a day.
3. Why would stopping the use of plastic bags cut back on oil use? Plastic is made from oil.

② **FLUENCY** **Record your progress on the Fluency Graph.**

My goal for reading the passage is ____ words per minute with two or fewer errors.

WORD LIST 19 -*ive*, -*ice*, -*ace*, -*ine*, and -*ain* Endings

-*ive* = /ĭv/	-*ice*, -*ace* = /ĭs/ or /əs/*	-*ine*, -*ain* = /ĭn/ or /ən/**	-*ine* = /ēn/
abusive	accomplice	bargain	chlorine
active	apprentice	captain	figurine
attractive	cowardice	certain	gasoline
captive	crevice	chaplain	machine
creative	furnace	chieftain	magazine
detective	grimace	curtain	marine
elective	justice	determine	mezzanine
expensive	menace	discipline	Pauline
fugitive	notice	doctrine	routine
massive	novice	engine	sardine
motive	office	examine	submarine
native	practice	famine	vaccine
negative	preface	feminine	
passive	prejudice	fountain	
perceptive	service	genuine	
positive	surface	imagine	
productive	terrace	Madeline	
relative	Wallace	masculine	
repulsive		medicine	
respective		mountain	
sensitive		porcelain	
		villain	

* These words can be pronounced both ways, /ĭs/ or /əs/. This lesson uses /ĭs/, but either pronunciation is correct.

** These words can be pronounced both ways, /ĭn/ or /ən/. This lesson uses /ĭn/, but either pronunciation is correct.

Practice Page 19A

-*ive*, -*ice*, -*ace*, -*ain*, and -*ine*

In single-syllable words, the endings -*ive*, -*ice*, -*ace*, -*ain*, and -*ine* have different long-vowel sounds.

In multisyllabic words, the endings -*ive*, -*ice*, -*ace*, -*ain*, and -*ine* usually have the same vowel sound, short-*i*.

Examples: *office, curtain*

① **Below are some final syllables of List 19 words. Read them aloud to practice the short-*i* sound.**

tive	nace	fice
sive	pline	tine
trine	tice	tain

Sometimes the ending -*ine* has a long-*e* sound. In these words, it says /ēn/.

Example: *machine*

② **Below are some final syllables of List 19 words. Read them aloud to practice the long-*e* sound.**

line   zine   dine

③ **Spell these List 19 endings.**

the ending that says /ĭv/ in multisyllabic words

ive

the endings that can say /ĭs/ in multisyllabic words

ice   ace

the endings that can say /ĭn/ in multisyllabic words

ain   ine

Practice Page 19B

/ĭs/ and /ĭn/

The unaccented ending /ĭs/ can be spelled either *-ice* or *-ace* as in *off__ice__* and *surf__ace__*.
The unaccented ending /ĭn/ can be spelled either *-ine* or *-ain* as in *eng__ine__* and *curt__ain__*.

1 Write two ways to spell the following unaccented syllables.

/lĭs/ might be spelled lice or lace.
/tĭn/ might be spelled tine or tain.
/gĭn/ might be spelled gine or gain.
/ĭs/ might be spelled ice or ace.
/fĭs/ might be spelled fice or face.

2 Fill in the blanks with *-ice* or *-ace*.

***-ice* = /ĭs/**	***-ace* = /ĭs/**
ac com pl ice	sur f ace
no t ice	ter r ace
of f ice	fur n ace
ser v ice	Wal l ace

3 Fill in the blanks with *-ine* or *-ain*.

***-ine* = /ĭn/**	***-ain* = /ĭn/**
fem i n ine	bar g ain
mas cu l ine	cap t ain
med i c ine	vil l ain
en g ine	

Practice Page 19C

Review

-ice and *-ace* are unaccented endings that have the same sound: /ĭs/ as in *office* and *surface*.

-ive

-ive is an unaccented ending that says /ĭv/ as in *active*.

1 Draw a box around the accented syllable. Say the syllables to read the whole word, and then write the word.

Accent the First Syllable

[ser] vice	service	[mo] tive	motive
[mas] sive	massive	[cap] tive	captive
[crev] ice	crevice	[pref] ace	preface
[no] tice	notice	[nov] ice	novice
[grim] ace	grimace	[men] ace	menace
[neg] a tive	negative	[fu] gi tive	fugitive
[rel] a tive	relative	[prej] u dice	prejudice
[cow] ar dice	cowardice	[sen] si tive	sensitive

Accent the Second Syllable

a [bu] sive	abusive	ap [pren] tice	apprentice
re [pul] sive	repulsive	ac [com] plice	accomplice
cre [a] tive	creative	pro [duc] tive	productive

Practice Page 19D

-ine and *-ain*

-ine and *-ain* are unaccented endings that have the same sound: /ĭn/ as in *engine* and *curtain*.

① **Draw a box around the accented syllable. Say the syllables to read the whole word, and then write the word.**

[fam] ine	famine	[vil] lain	villain
[doc] trine	doctrine	[chap] lain	chaplain
[dis] ci pline	discipline	[por] ce lain	porcelain
[gen] u ine	genuine	de [ter] mine	determine
[mas] cu line	masculine	im [a] gine	imagine
ex [am] ine	examine	[fem] i nine	feminine

-ine also says /ēn/ as in *machine*. In two-syllable words that end with /ēn/, the final syllable has the accent. In three-syllable words that end with /ēn/, the first syllable has the primary accent and the final syllable has a secondary accent.

② **Draw a box around the syllable with the primary accent and underline the syllable with the secondary accent, if applicable. Say the syllables to read the whole word, and then write the word.**

ma [rine]	marine	[mag] a <u>zine</u>	magazine
rou [tine]	routine	[mez] za <u>nine</u>	mezzanine
sar [dine]	sardine	[sub] ma <u>rine</u>	submarine

Review

-ine is unaccented when it says /___ĭn___/.

-ine is accented when it says /___ēn___/.

Practice Page 19E

① **Your teacher will dictate fourteen words. Spell the missing syllable(s). Then say the whole word as you write it.**

1.	ac	tive		active
2.	cap	tive		captive
3.	rel	a	tive	relative
4.	pos	i	tive	positive
5.	of	fice		office
6.	cow	ar	dice	cowardice
7.	fur	nace		furnace
8.	fam	ine		famine
9.	fem	i	nine	feminine
10.	de	ter	mine	determine
11.	med	i	cine	medicine
12.	bar	gain		bargain
13.	sar	dine		sardine
14.	gas	o	line	gasoline

② **Fill in the blanks with *-ive*, *-ice*, or *-ine*. Then write the whole word.**

at trac t ive	attractive
re spec t ive	respective
no t ice	notice
ex am ine	examine
gen u ine	genuine
im a g ine	imagine

Practice Page 19F

① Read each word aloud, and listen for the accented syllable. Then write the words syllable by syllable under the correct headings.

native	positive	sardine	productive
machine	mountain	negative	detective
office	masculine	expensive	routine
menace	discipline	engine	attractive
marine	medicine	respective	vaccine

Two-Syllable Words

na	tive
of	fice
men	ace
moun	tain
en	gine
ma	chine
ma	rine
sar	dine
vac	cine
rou	tine

Three-Syllable Words

pos	i	tive
mas	cu	line
dis	ci	pline
med	i	cine
neg	a	tive
ex	pen	sive
res	pec	tive
pro	duc	tive
at	trac	tive
de	tec	tive

Practice Page 19G

Review

Sometimes *-ine* is unaccented and says /ĭn/ as in *engine*.
Other times *-ine* says /ēn/ as in *magazine*.

① Write the words under the correct headings.

marine	medicine	examine	Pauline
doctrine	gasoline	chlorine	engine
genuine	machine	determine	masculine
sardine	discipline	magazine	feminine
submarine	routine	vaccine	imagine

***-ine* = /ĭn/**	***-ine* = /ēn/**
doctrine	marine
genuine	sardine
medicine	submarine
discipline	gasoline
examine	machine
determine	routine
engine	chlorine
masculine	magazine
feminine	vaccine
imagine	Pauline

② **QUICK CHECK** Have another student test you on spelling these words.

My score: ____/____ words correct

Practice Page 19H

Review

The unaccented endings *-ine* and *-ain* occur in final syllables and have the same sound: /ĭn/.

① **Fill in the blanks with the correct *-ine* or *-ain* ending. Then write the whole word.**

eng_ine_	engine
capt_ain_	captain
curt_ain_	curtain
femin_ine_	feminine
exam_ine_	examine
vill_ain_	villain
barg_ain_	bargain
cert_ain_	certain
mascul_ine_	masculine
genu_ine_	genuine
discipl_ine_	discipline
mount_ain_	mountain
determ_ine_	determine
fount_ain_	fountain

② **QUICK CHECK** **Have another student test you on spelling these words.**

My score: ____/____ words correct

Practice Page 19I

Review

The unaccented endings *-ice* and *-ace* have the same sound: /ĭs/.

① **Write the words in the box under the correct headings.**

office	furnace	practice	notice
surface	justice	service	menace
preface	cowardice	terrace	prejudice

***-ice* = /ĭs/**	***-ace* = /ĭs/**
office	surface
justice	preface
cowardice	furnace
practice	terrace
service	menace
notice	
prejudice	

② **EXCEPTION** **Most multisyllabic words that end in *-ice* have the accent on the first syllable. The word *police* is an exception because the accent is on the final syllable. Say the word *police*. Write it on the lines.**

police   police

Does the ending say /ĭs/, /əs/, or /ēs/? /_ēs_/

Practice Page 19J

① Write the words syllable by syllable under the correct headings.

active	service	practice	negative	gasoline
relative	machine	expensive	engine	routine
office	furnace	surface	medicine	magazine
massive	captive	certain	bargain	apprentice
prejudice	accomplice	mountain	chieftain	terrace

-ive

	ac	tive
	mas	sive
	cap	tive
rel	a	tive
ex	pen	sive
neg	a	tive

-ine

	ma	chine
	en	gine
	rou	tine
med	i	cine
gas	o	line
mag	a	zine

-ain

cer	tain
moun	tain
bar	gain
chief	tain

-ace

fur	nace
sur	face
ter	race

-ice

	of	fice
	ser	vice
	prac	tice
prej	u	dice
ac	com	plice
ap	pren	tice

Practice Page 19K

① Write the words in the box under the correct headings.

gasoline	routine	bargain	masculine
genuine	sardine	villain	curtain
imagine	famine	vaccine	certain

***-ine* = /ēn/**	***-ine* = /ĭn/**	***-ain* = /ĭn/**
gasoline	genuine	bargain
routine	imagine	villain
sardine	famine	curtain
vaccine	masculine	certain

② **Read the definitions. Choose the correct word from Activity 1, and write it on the line.**

a small fish preserved in oil	sardine
a fixed and regular method of doing things; a habit	routine
opposite of feminine	masculine
a good deal; an agreement to trade	bargain
medicine to prevent sickness, usually given as a shot	vaccine
a fuel for cars	gasoline
known for sure; fixed; settled	certain
real; not fake	genuine
to use your imagination	imagine
fabric over or around a window	curtain
the evil person in a story	villain
a lack of food; a time of starvation	famine

Practice Page 19L

① **Fill in the blanks with words from the box.**

positive	detective	attractive	relative
captive	motive	massive	sensitive
expensive	negative	passive	active

1. The bandits held him ___captive___ for ten days.
2. The ___detective___ solved the crime before the police officers did.
3. These diamonds are very ___expensive___. They cost twice as much as the pearls.
4. Uncle Dan is the only ___relative___ I have who lives in Florida.
5. Bernice is quite ___passive___. She never does anything active.
6. The boulder was so ___massive___ that it took two bulldozers to move it.
7. Was the ___motive___ for the crime revenge or profit?
8. Jamal is quite ___active___. He never sits down.
9. Please pull the shades down; my eyes are ___sensitive___ to light.
10. Mona Lisa was an ___attractive___ woman; her portrait is pleasing to the eye.
11. Being ___negative___ all the time is depressing. Be ___positive___ instead!

Practice Page 19M

Review

Nouns are words that refer to people, places, things, or ideas.

① **Read the definitions. Choose the correct nouns in the box, and write it on the line.**

accomplice	preface	fugitive	crevice
apprentice	novice	grimace	

a beginner; one who is new at what they are doing	novice
a person who is learning a trade, profession, or art	apprentice
a narrow split or crack	crevice
a person who shares in the guilt for a crime	accomplice
an introduction to a book	preface
a person who is running away or trying to escape	fugitive
a look of disgust or disapproval	grimace

② **Fill in the blanks with words from Activity 1.**

1. The mountain climber lost his footing when he stepped into a ___crevice___.
2. Wallace was a ___novice___ at snowboarding even though he's been skiing for six years.
3. My grandmother made a ___grimace___ when I talked about getting a tattoo.
4. The villain is a ___fugitive___ from the law and never stays in one place for long.
5. The ___preface___ describes how the author got inspired to write the book.
6. Mel wants to become an electrician's ___apprentice___ so she can learn the trade hands-on.
7. The ___accomplice___ was fined $50,000 for advising how to profit from an Internet scam.

Practice Page 19N

Review

A *noun* is a word that refers to a person, place, thing, or idea.
A *verb* is a word that shows action.
An *adjective* is a word that describes a noun.

1 Write the words in the box under the correct headings.

fugitive	apprentice	massive	captain
determine	furnace	imagine	sardine
repulsive	examine	engine	detective
medicine	practice	masculine	abusive

Nouns (things)	Nouns (people)	Verbs	Adjectives
medicine	fugitive	determine	repulsive
furnace	apprentice	examine	massive
engine	captain	practice	masculine
sardine	detective	imagine	abusive

2 Write five sentences. Use at least three words from Activity 1 in each sentence.

1. Answers will vary.
2.
3.
4.
5.

Practice Page 19O

1 Read the paragraphs. Underline the words that end with *-ine, -ice, -ive,* and *-ain*.

Paragraph 1

I imagine that the doctor has an active practice in the hospital. I notice that, as a routine, he will examine people and provide them with vaccines. If a negative reaction occurs, the person is probably sensitive to the medicine.

Paragraph 2

Pauline was a novice detective, but she was perceptive in most matters. She told her captain that the marine must have had an accomplice who was a machine operator and a native of the mountains.

2 Write the words you underlined in Activity 1 under the correct headings.

-ine = /ĭn/	*-ine* = /ēn/	*-ice* = /ĭs/
imagine	routine	practice
examine	vaccine	notice
medicine	Pauline	novice
	marine	accomplice
	machine	

-ive = /ĭv/	*-ain* = /ĭn/
active	captain
negative	mountain
sensitive	
detective	
perceptive	
native	

Practice Page 19P

Proofreading Practice

Two of the List 19 words are misspelled in each sentence. Rewrite the whole sentence, and spell the words correctly.

1. Madeline could not determin if the diamonds were genuin.
   Madeline could not determine if the diamonds were genuine.
2. The marene was taken captiv during the riots in his native country.
   The marine was taken captive during the riots in his native country.
3. The detektive was certain that Wallace had been an accomplace to the crime.
   The detective was certain that Wallace had been an accomplice to the crime.
4. The repulsive movie villian was a menace who made me grimice.
   The repulsive movie villain was a menace who made me grimace.
5. Our rutine mountain drive turned into a nightmare when we ran out of gasoleen.
   Our routine mountain drive turned into a nightmare when we ran out of gasoline.
6. The novice apprentise practiced using all the masheens in the shop.
   The novice apprentice practiced using all the machines in the shop.
7. In the prefice, the author of this book examined his creativ process.
   In the preface, the author of this book examined his creative process.
8. The captain guided the submerrine to the surface better than we imajined.
   The captain guided the submarine to the surface better than we imagined.

Practice Page 19Q

① Read the sentences and circle all the List 19 words.

1. While engaged in a routine mission, the marine was taken captive by the natives.
2. The solar-powered engine was an expensive machine.
3. Did you notice the gasoline fumes around the furnace?
4. Ask the service station attendant to examine the car's engine.
5. The police detective brought the villain to justice.
6. Massive doses of the medicine cured the illness.
7. The apprentice needed to practice running the office machines.
8. The velvet curtains we bought for the chaplain's office were certainly no bargain.
9. The attractive figurine was more masculine than feminine.
10. Pauline uses genuine gold and porcelain crowns in her dental practice.
11. The sensitive chaplain made a grimace when we talked about the famine in Sudan.
12. Captain Wallace gave the novice recruits information on the dangers of prejudice.
13. The repulsive fugitive was determined to escape in the submarine.

② Your teacher will dictate three of the sentences above. Write them on a blank piece of paper.

③ Write a short story or descriptive paragraph using ten words from List 19. Be creative!

Reading & Spelling Skill Check

Demonstrate your accuracy in reading and spelling List 19 words. Your teacher will select ten words to read and ten words to spell. Record your scores on the Accuracy Checklist. Work toward 90–100 percent accuracy.

Word Proficiency

Now build up your reading proficiency with List 19 words. Decide on your rate goal with your teacher. Record your progress on the Word Proficiency Graph.

My goal for reading List 19 is ________ words per minute with two or fewer errors.

Practice Page 19R

① Practice the words, read the passage, and then answer the questions.

List 19 Words			Review Words		Passage Words
expensive	masculine	grimace	latest	offer	bicycle
positive	notice	detective	number	hundred	answered
bargain	attractive		skeptical	murmured	police
office	machines				

A Real Bargain?

Ross slammed on his bicycle brakes to read a sign.

Are you sick of paying expensive prices for the latest Game Box system? I am positive I can get you a bargain.

The sign listed an office phone number. Ross was skeptical, but he pulled out his cell phone and made the call.

A masculine voice answered the phone.

"I saw your notice for Game Boxes," said Ross. "Do you have an attractive offer?"

"These machines are a steal—I mean, a *deal*—at five hundred bucks each," murmured the voice on the other end.

Ross made a grimace when he heard the price. "That's hardly a bargain!" he said. "But maybe I'll swing by your office, with my uncle. He's a big gamer… and a police detective."

The line went dead. "Funny," Ross thought, as he called his uncle. "Now he'll be making another deal—with the police."

1. Which word from the text means "a very good deal"? bargain
2. Why did Ross call the number? He wanted to buy a Game Box system for a low price.
3. Why will the man on the phone want to make a deal with the police? He might be doing something illegal with the Game Box systems.

② **FLUENCY Decide on your fluency rate goal with your teacher. Record your progress on the Fluency Graph.**

My goal for reading the passage is ____ words per minute with two or fewer errors.

REVIEW LIST 15–19

abdomen	determine	granite	occupant	relative
absent	diet	hospital	octopus	removal
accurate	different	ignorant	opposite	residence
ambulance	diplomat	important	oral	reversal
arrival	elastic	influence	panic	sarcastic
Atlantic	entrance	inhabit	permanent	several
attendance	envelope	innocent	picnic	silent
benefit	fantastic	insurance	plastic	singular
captain	feminine	justice	pocket	terrific
captive	final	limit	porcupine	toilet
certain	fortunate	magazine	positive	vacant
certificate	fountain	manager	practice	vaccinate
chocolate	frequent	market	prejudice	vaccine
comedy	furnace	masculine	present	velvet
concentrate	garlic	moderate	president	villain
definite	gasoline	natural	profit	violent
democrat	gigantic	notice		

Review List 15–19

1. **Unscramble the syllables to make real words.**

da nce ten at	attendance
gan gi tic	gigantic
in ence flu	influence
er mod ate	moderate
con trate cen	concentrate
sal re ver	reversal
line mas cu	masculine
i tive pos	positive

2. **Underline the word that is spelled correctly.**

1. Jillian waited for her friends to join her at the *(entrance, entrence)* of the movie theater.
2. Lucas felt *(fortunite, fortunate)* to be chosen as team captain.
3. An ambulance brought Felicia to the *(hospitel, hospital)* for evaluation after the car accident.
4. The *(innocent, innosant)* man was confident the jury would find him not guilty.
5. When you remove a file from your computer, you get a warning that the removal is *(permanant, permanent)*; the file cannot be retrieved.
6. One *(relative, relativ)* I hadn't met until this week is my Aunt Sophia.
7. As a special treat, Mom made a three-layer *(chocolite, chocolate)* cake.
8. Philip has a *(terrific, terrifec)* idea to help us raise the money for our field trip.

Review List 15–19

3. **Write the words in the box under the correct headings.**

ambulance	determine	certificate	inhabit
sarcastic	fountain	president	several
vaccinate	fantastic	diplomat	silent
captain	furnace	concentrate	captive

Nouns (things)	Nouns (people)
ambulance	captain
fountain	president
furnace	diplomat
certificate	captive

Verbs	Adjectives
vaccinate	sarcastic
determine	fantastic
concentrate	several
inhabit	silent

4. **Write four sentences. Use at least three words from Activity 3 in each sentence.**

1. Answers will vary.
2.
3.
4.

Review List 15–19

(5) **Read the definitions. Choose the correct word from the box, and write it on the line.**

absent	frequent	natural	elastic	justice
benefit	envelope	limit	market	diet

a stretchable material	elastic
often, regularly	frequent
the amount allowed	limit
having to do with nature	natural
an eating plan	diet
something that helps; to help	benefit
something that holds a letter	envelope
not present	absent
a store that sells food	market
fairness in the way people are treated	justice

(6) **Fill in the blanks with words from the box.**

important	arrival	different	furnace	vacant

1. The ad said there is a ___vacant___ apartment for rent nearby.
2. We cooked many ___different___ foods for the banquet; everyone should be able to find something they like.
3. Our ___arrival___ back home was delayed by four hours.
4. We have no hot water for our shower right now because our ___furnace___ is broken.
5. After such a terrible car accident, the most ___important___ thing was that everyone was okay.

List 15 **Reading Skill Check, Form A**

Name ______________________ **Date** ______________

natural	allergic
mystic	federal
electric	mineral
final	music
structural	terrific

List 15 **Reading Skill Check, Form B**

Name ______________________ **Date** ______________

several	traffic
tidal	skeptical
democratic	patriotic
basic	metal
local	skeptic

List 15 **Recording Form for Practice Page 15P**

Name ______________________________ **Date** ____________________

List 15 Words			Review Words	Passage Words	
naval	Atlantic	dismal	hero	African	Louis
Royal	loyal	central	members	American(s)	businessman
coastal	patriotic			parents	figure

James Forten 2

James Forten was an African American hero. He was born to 13
free parents in 1766—a time when few black Americans were 24
free. When James was ten, Americans went to war to be free of 37
British rule. 39

At the age of fourteen, James went to serve on a naval ship, 52
the Royal Louis. The ship sailed along the coastal shores and 63
cruised the Atlantic. James worked as a powder boy. His job was 75
to bring gun powder to the ship's large guns. 84

One day a British ship took over James's ship. Most of the 96
time, when the British took over a ship, they sold black crew 108
members as slaves. But James made friends on the British ship. 119
The British told him they would free him if he swore to be loyal 133
to their side. James was too patriotic and said no. So the British 146
kept him for seven dismal months. 152

James was let go after the war. He became a wealthy 163
businessman, and he used his wealth to help fellow blacks. 173
While not a central figure in the war, James is a central figure in 187
African American history. 190

Fluency Rate

__________ − __________ = __________

Words read in 1 minute | Errors | WCPM

List 16

Reading Skill Check, Form A

Name ______________________ **Date** ______________

opposite	private
climate	credit
approximate	planet
diet	separate
deposit	congratulate

List 16

Reading Skill Check, Form B

Name ______________________ **Date** ______________

definite	pocket
market	chocolate
prohibit	concentrate
debit	target
senate	habit

Name ______________________ **Date** ______________

List 16 Words		Review Words		Passage Words	
rockets	immaculate	program	person	American	satellite
candidates	orbit	until	later	woman	around
definite	fortunate	people	doctor	image	mission
prohibited	planet	started	studied	photos	Jemison
toilets	climate	ideas		Sullivan	African

Space Firsts for American Women 5

Sally Ride was the first American woman in space. She 15
was part of the space shuttle program. Until 1981, rockets 25
took people into space. In 1978, candidates started training 34
for shuttle flight. Ride's first flight was in 1983. 43

Ride had definite ideas about her image. She prohibited 52
photos of her fixing food or cleaning toilets. Every person on 63
a shuttle crew did those tasks, but she felt the world should 75
see her doing more than making the shuttle immaculate. 84

A year later, Kathy Sullivan became the first American 93
woman to walk in space. She worked on a satellite that was in 106
orbit around Earth. In 1992, she was fortunate to join the first 118
mission to study our planet's climate from space. 126

That same year, Mae Jemison became the first African 135
American woman in space. Jemison was a doctor. On her 145
mission, she studied how bones grow in space. 153

Fluency Rate

________ − ________ = ________

Words read in 1 minute — Errors — WCPM

List 17

Reading Skill Check, Form A

Name ____________________ Date ____________

benefit
chocolate
alphabet
calculate
envelope

octopus
customer
complement
pharmacy
stimulate

List 17

Reading Skill Check, Form B

Name ____________________ Date ____________

occupy
Canada
remedy
persecute
relative

innocent
absolute
singular
elephant
balcony

List 17

Recording Form for Practice Page 170

Name ______________________ **Date** ______________

List 17 Words			Review Words		Passage Words	
octopus	tentacles	calculate	elastic	study	invertebrate	feature
acrobat	enemy	alphabet	largest	learned	water	family
relative	singular	perseveres	problem	until	hungry	scientists
						solving

A Smart Invertebrate? 3

The octopus is an invertebrate, which means it has no 13
bones. It moves through the water like an elastic acrobat. 23
Like its relative the squid, it has eight tentacles. It can shoot 35
out a cloud of black ink at a hungry enemy. Some types of 48
octopus can kill humans or even sharks. 55

But the most singular feature of an octopus may be 65
its brain. The octopus seems to be very smart—for an 76
invertebrate. In fact, the octopus has the largest brain in 86
the boneless family. It can't calculate square roots or learn 96
the alphabet. But scientists have found it can do easy 106
problem solving. 108

One study showed that the octopus can tell shapes 117
apart. Another study showed it can learn to play with toys. An 128
octopus in a German zoo even learned to twist the top 140
off a food jar. It perseveres up to an hour until the lid is off. 155

Fluency Rate

______ − ______ = ______

Words read in 1 minute — Errors — WCPM

Reading Skill Check, Form A

Name ______________________________ **Date** ________________

balcony	separate
original	climate
remedy	argument
indefinite	central
compromise	deliberate

- -

List 15–17

Reading Skill Check, Form B

Name ______________________________ **Date** ________________

electric	customer
manager	central
immediate	planet
music	plural
donate	abdomen

Reading Skill Check, Form A

Name ______________________________ **Date** ________________

excellent	frequent
ambulance	correspondent
significant	preference
violence	truancy
defiance	distant

List 18

Reading Skill Check, Form B

Name ______________________________ **Date** ________________

innocent	silence
decency	acceptance
difference	infant
ignorant	obedient
evident	insurance

List 18 **Recording Form for Practice Page 18R**

Name ______________________ **Date** ______________

List 18 Words		Review Words		Passage Words	
dependent	important	everyone	fuels	energy	barrels
significant	dependence	plastic	prepare	supply	because
abundant	frequency	never		million	hydrogen
constant	appliances				
recent	excellent				

Cutting Dependence on Oil 4

The U.S. is dependent on oil for most of its energy. Why 16
is this significant? Because what was once an abundant and 26
constant supply will dry up one day. 33

In recent years, the U.S. has used close to twenty million 44
barrels of oil a day. It is now important for everyone to make 57
smart choices about energy use to cut dependence on oil. 67

We can cut back on the frequency of our oil use. We can 80
use bikes and not cars. We can turn down home heaters and 92
use appliances that burn less oil. Even stopping the use of 103
plastic bags can help because plastic is made from oil. 113

We will need to find new forms of energy, too. Sun and 125
wind power are excellent choices because they are abundant 134
and will never run out. New car fuels such as hydrogen may 146
also help. Smart choices now will prepare us for the future. 157

Fluency Rate

______ − ______ = ______

Words read in 1 minute — Errors = WCPM

List 19 Reading Skill Check, Form A

Name ______________________ Date ______________

bargain
curtain
doctrine
passive
sensitive
terrace
relative
gasoline
figurine
furnace

List 19 Reading Skill Check, Form B

Name ______________________ Date ______________

elective
discipline
famine
active
apprentice
magazine
submarine
justice
imagine
repulsive

List 19

Recording Form for Practice Page 19R

Name ______________________ **Date** ______________

List 19 Words			Review Words		Passage Words
expensive	masculine	grimace	latest	offer	bicycle
positive	notice	detective	number	hundred	answered
bargain	attractive		skeptical	murmured	police
office	machines				

A Real Bargain? 3

Ross slammed on his bicycle brakes to read a sign. 13

Are you sick of paying expensive prices for the latest Game 24
Box system? I am positive I can get you a bargain. 35

The sign listed an office phone number. Ross was 44
skeptical, but he pulled out his cell phone and made the call. 56

A masculine voice answered the phone. 62

"I saw your notice for Game Boxes," said Ross. "Do you 73
have an attractive offer?" 77

"These machines are a steal—I mean, a *deal*—at five 88
hundred bucks each," murmured the voice on the other end. 98

Ross made a grimace when he heard the price. "That's 108
hardly a bargain!" he said. "But maybe I'll swing by your office, 120
with my uncle. He's a big gamer... and a police detective." 131

The line went dead. "Funny," Ross thought, as he called his 142
uncle. "Now he'll be making another deal—with the police." 152

Fluency Rate

______	−	______	=	______
Words read in 1 minute		Errors		WCPM

Review List 15–19 **Reading Skill Check, Form A**

Name ______________________ **Date** ______________

prejudice	concentrate
chocolate	elastic
violent	fountain
vaccine	natural
pocket	envelope

Review List 15–19 **Reading Skill Check, Form B**

Name ______________________ **Date** ______________

octopus	president
gigantic	manager
moderate	several
captain	absent
insurance	velvet

List ____

Spelling Skill Check

Name ______________________________ **Date** ________________

1. ______________________________
2. ______________________________
3. ______________________________
4. ______________________________
5. ______________________________
6. ______________________________
7. ______________________________
8. ______________________________
9. ______________________________
10. ______________________________

Syllable Types and Syllabication Rules

The Six Types of Syllables

Closed (VC) — A closed syllable has only one vowel and ends in a consonant. The vowel is usually short: *ad, sug, lish, trom, ject.*

Silent-*e* (VC*e*) — A silent-*e* syllable has one vowel followed by a consonant followed by an *e*. The *e* is silent and makes the preceding vowel long: *plete, mune, stroke, ope, mate.*

Open (CV) — An open syllable ends in one vowel. The vowel is usually long: *pi, glo, stri, u, cy, re.*

***r*-Controlled (V*r*)** — An *r*-controlled syllable has a vowel followed by an *r*, which modifies the vowel sound: *car, mer, fir, cor, tur.*

Consonant-*le* (C*le*) — A consonant-*le* syllable is a final syllable in which the *e* is silent; thus it sounds like consonant-*əl*: *ta-ble, jun-gle, sim-ple, bu-gle.*

Double-Vowel (VV) — A double-vowel syllable has two vowels that together make one sound. This sound has to be learned, as it often takes on a sound different from either single vowel: *boat, fie, haul, voy, floun.*

The Five Syllabication Rules

VC/CV — When two or more consonants stand between two vowels, divide between the consonants, so that consonant blends and digraphs stay together: *pup-pet, hun-dred, sup-pose, fan-tas-tic.*

V/CV — When a single consonant is surrounded by two vowels, you usually divide the word into syllables before the consonant, making the vowel in the first syllable long: *hu-man, lo-cate, pi-lot, e-ven.*

VC/V — If the V/CV Syllabication Rule doesn't make a real word, divide the syllables after the consonant, and give the vowel its short sound: *rap-id, sol-id, cab-in, stud-y.*

/C*le* — Divide the syllables before the consonant-*le*. Count three letters from the end of the word and divide: *star-tle, sta-ble, ea-gle.*

V/V — Divide only a few words between the vowels. The vowel in the first syllable is always long: *di-et, flu-id, qui-et, i-o-dine.*

Summary of Accent Patterns

Accented Syllable—An accented syllable is pronounced as if it were a one-syllable word with a clear vowel sound according to its syllabic type *(ac´ tive, com plete´, ser´ vant, loy´ al).*

Unaccented Syllable—An unaccented syllable is pronounced with a schwa /ə/ or short-*i* /ĭ/ vowel sound regardless of its syllabic type *(rib´ bon, op´ po site, in de pen´ dent).*

Accent Patterns—The dark lines and accent marks in this book are accent patterns (___´ ___). Each line stands for one syllable. The accent mark shows which syllable is accented. Learning to place the accent on the proper syllable will help you recognize most multisyllabic words. The accent patterns below will help you determine which syllable in a word is accented.

Primary Accent—A strong stress on a syllable in a multisyllabic word.

Secondary Accent—A weaker stress on a syllable in a multisyllabic word.

General Guideline—In two- and three-syllable words, accent the first syllable. Then pronounce the first vowel as if it were a short, long, *r*-controlled, or double-vowel sound in a one-syllable word. If that doesn't make a recognizable word, accent the second syllable, and pronounce the second vowel according to its syllabic type.

Accent Patterns for Two-Syllable Words

1. **Accent on the first syllable (___´ ___)**
   The accent is usually on the first syllable in two-syllable words *(stan´ dard, sis´ ter, dol´ lar).*
2. **Accent on the second syllable (___ ___´)**
   Two-syllable words that have a prefix in the first syllable and a root in the second syllable are usually accented on the second syllable *(ex tend´, con fuse´).*
3. **Accent on either the first or second syllable (___´ ___ or ___ ___´)**
   If a word can function as both noun and verb, the noun is accented on the prefix *(con´ duct)* and the verb is accented on the root *(con duct´).*

Accent Patterns for Three-Syllable Words

1. **Accent on the first syllable (___´ ___ ___)**
   The accent is usually on the first syllable in three-syllable words. The unaccented middle syllable has a schwa sound *(vis´ i tor, char´ ac ter).*
2. **Accent on the second syllable (___ ___´ ___)**
   The accent is usually on the second syllable (the root) in words that contain a prefix, root, and suffix *(de stroy´ er, in ven´ tor).*

Accent Patterns for Four-Syllable Words (___ ___´ ___ ___)

1. The accent is usually on the second syllable in four-syllable words *(in tel´ li gence, sig nif´ i cant).*

Special Accent Patterns for Words of Three or More Syllables

Accent patterns for words longer than two syllables are often governed by a specific ending pattern or an unaccented vowel.

1. **Accent with the ending -ic**
   Accent the syllable just before the ending *-ic (e las´ tic, en er get´ ic, char ac ter is´ tic).*

2. **Accent with the ending -ate /āt/**
   In three-syllable words, the first syllable has a primary accent and *-ate* has a secondary accent *(vi´ o late´).*
   In four-syllable words, the second syllable has a primary accent and *-ate* has a secondary accent *(con grat´ u late´).*

3. **Accent with schwa endings**
   Schwa endings (and schwa syllables) are never accented. The accent falls on another syllable in the word *(in´ no cent, ex ter´ nal, ap pren´ tice).*

4. **Accent with the endings -tion, -sion, -cian**
   Accent the syllable just before the endings *-tion, -sion,* and *-cian (pol lu´ tion, im pres´ sion, ad min is tra´ tion, e lec tri´ cian).*

5. **Accent with the ending -ity /ĭ tē/**
   Accent the syllable just before the ending *-ity (qual´ i ty, ac tiv´ i ty, per son al´ i ty).*

6. **Accent in words with an unaccented middle syllable**
   Accent the syllable just before the unaccented middle syllable with *i* as /ə/, *i* as /ē/, and *u* as /ə/ or /ū/ *(sim´ i lar, aud´ i ence, par tic´ u lar).*

7. **Accent in words with i as /y/**
   Accent the syllable just before the unaccented syllable with *i* as /y/ *(com pan´ ion, in con ven´ ient, mem or a bil´ ia).*

8. **Accent in words with *ti* or *ci* as /sh/**
   Accent the syllable just before a final syllable with *ti* or *ci* as /sh/ *(fi nan´ cial, pres i den´ tial).*

Accuracy Checklist

***Megawords 3,* Lists 15–19**

Name ______________________________

Word List	Examples	Check Test Scores Date:		Reading Skill Check			Spelling Skill Check		
		Reading	**Spelling**						
15. *-al* and *-ic* Endings	eternal athletic								
16. *-it*, *-ite*, *-et*, and *-ate* Endings	audit closet opposite private								
17. Middle-Syllable Schwa	antelope chocolate								
Review List: 15–17									
18. *-ant*, *-ance*, *-ent*, and *-ence* Endings	important balance different absence								
19. *-ive*, *-ice*, *-ace*, *-ine*, and *-ain* Endings	examine sensitive								
Review List: 15–19									

Record scores as fractions: $\frac{\text{\# correct}}{\text{\# attempted}}$

Word Proficiency Graph

Name ______________________________

Goal ______________________________

•———• Words read correctly in one minute (WCPM)

×———× Errors

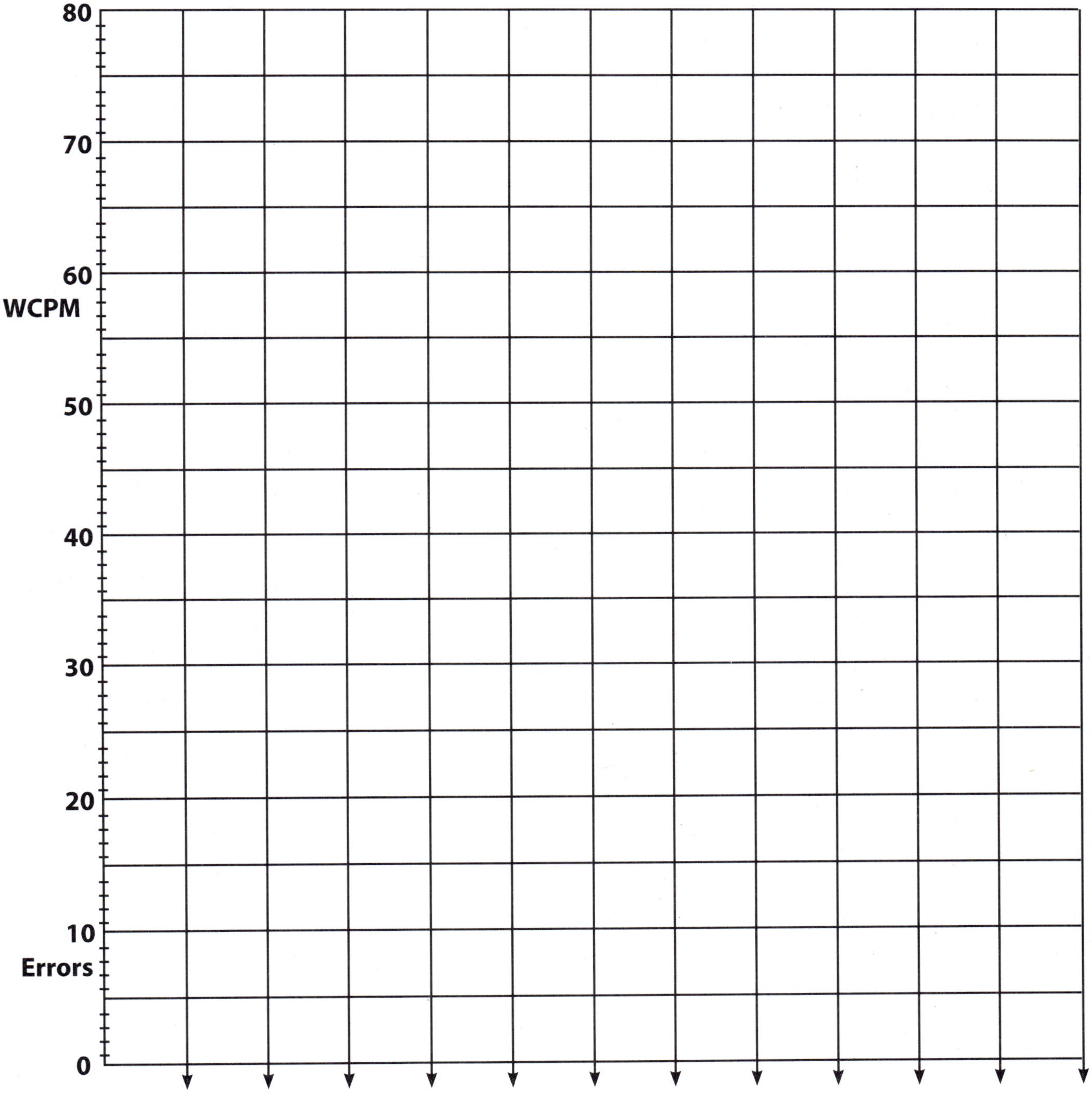

Word List* ______________________________

Date ______________________________

Errors ______________________________

WCPM** ______________________________

*Repeat Word Lists as many times as needed.

**Word Count Per Minute (WCPM) = Words read in one minute - Errors

Fluency Graph

Name ______________________________

Goal ______________________________

●———● Words read correctly in one minute (WCPM)

×———× Errors

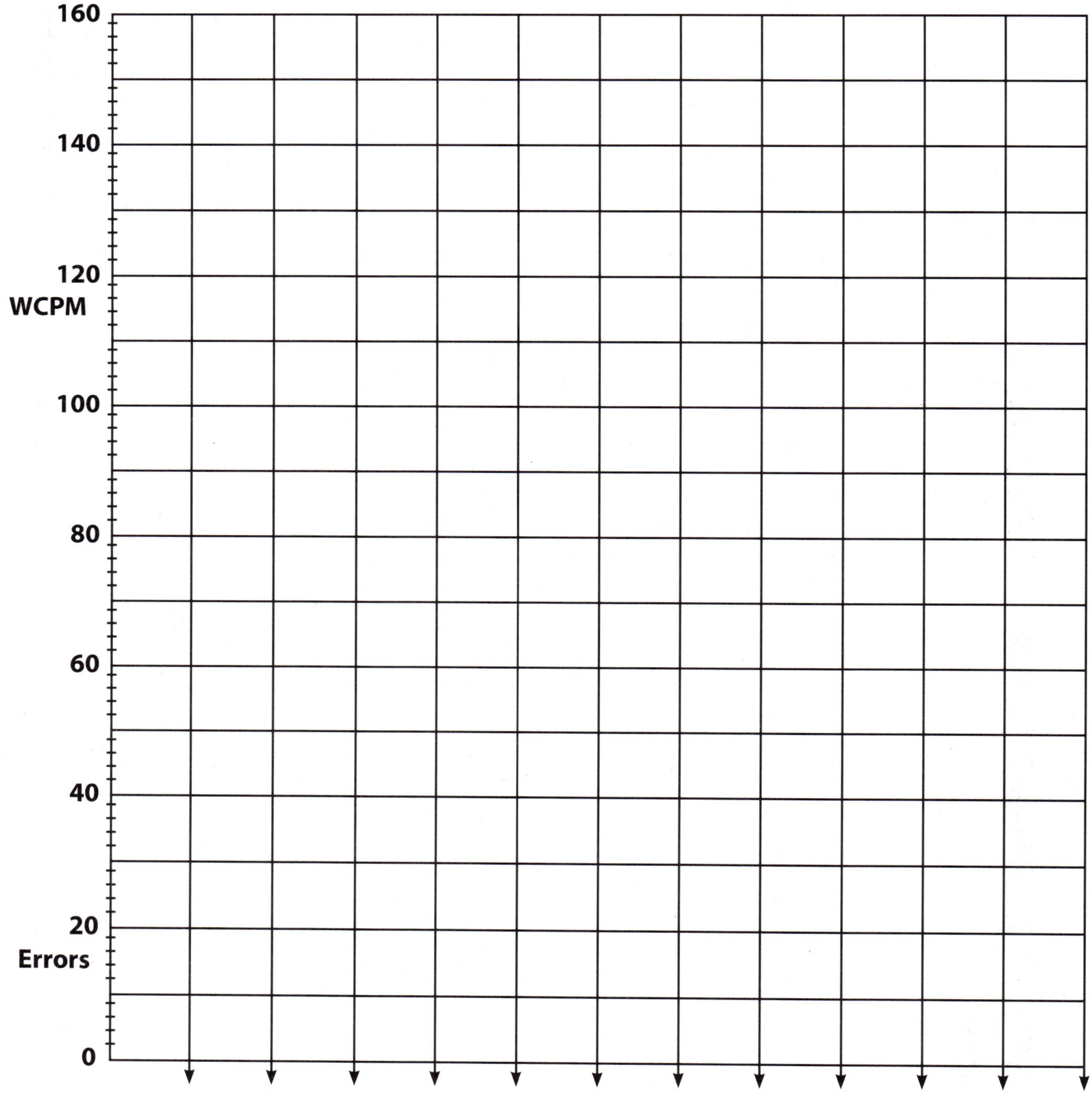

Passage* ______________________________

Date ______________________________

Errors ______________________________

WCPM** ______________________________

* Repeat Passages as many times as needed.

**Word Count Per Minute (WCPM) = Words read in one minute - Errors

EXAMINER'S RECORDING FORM — READING

Check Test: Lists 15–19

Megawords 3

Name ______________________ Date ______________________

15. *-al* and *-ic* Endings

reversal
frantic
electric
interval
loyal
correct ________

16. *-it*, *-ite*, *-et*, and *-ate* Endings

delicate
velvet
favorite
deposit
moderate
correct ________

17. Middle-Syllable Schwa

execute
buffalo
balcony
singular
emphasize
correct ________

18. *-ant*, *-ance*, *-ent*, and *-ence* Endings

ignorant
resistance
resident
presence
attendance
correct ________

19. *-ive*, *-ice*, *-ace*, *-ine*, and *-ain* Endings

masculine
practice
detective
certain
magazine
correct ________

Total Correct ________

Total Possible 25

STUDENT'S READING COPY

Check Test: Lists 15–19

Megawords 3

15. reversal
    frantic
    electric
    interval
    loyal

16. delicate
    velvet
    favorite
    deposit
    moderate

17. execute
    buffalo
    balcony
    singular
    emphasize

18. objectionable
    occasionally
    opportunity
    disagreement
    distinguished

19. masculine
    practice
    detective
    certain
    magazine